BIG BOOK OF SPORTS QUOTES

BIG BOOK OF
SPORTS

QUOTES

COMPILED BY
Eric Zweig AND
Chris McDonell

FIREFLY BOOKS

A Firefly Book

Published by Firefly Books Ltd. 2010

Compiled by Eric Zweig and Chris McDonell

The publisher gratefully acknowledges the financial support for our publishing program by the Government of Canada
through the Canada Book Fund as administered by the Department of Canadian Heritage.

First printing

Library and Archives Canada Cataloguing in Publication
Zweig, Eric, 1963-
    Big book of sports quotes / Eric Zweig and Chris
McDonell.
ISBN-13: 978-1-55407-650-5
ISBN-10: 1-55407-650-1
1. Athletes--Quotations. 2. Sports--Quotations, maxims, etc.
I. McDonell, Chris, 1960- II. Title.
GV706.8.Z83 2010   796   C2010-901869-9

Publisher Cataloging-in-Publication Data (U.S.)
Zweig, Eric.
    The big book of sports quotes / Eric Zweig and Chris
McDonell.
[ ] p. : photos. ; cm.
summary: 1,000 amusing quotations and 100 matching
photographs of great stars from baseball, football, golf,
basketball and hockey.
ISBN-13: 978-155407-650-5
ISBN-10: 1-55407-650-1
1. Sports—Quotations, maxims, etc. I. McDonell, Chris.
II. Title.
796 dc22 GV706.8.Z94   2010

Published in Canada by
Firefly Books Ltd.
66 Leek Crescent
Richmond Hill, Ontario L4B 1H1

Published in the United States by
Firefly Books (U.S.) Inc.
P.O. Box 1338, Ellicott Station
Buffalo, New York 14205

Cover and interior design: Sonya V. Thursby, opushouse.com

Printed in China

CONTENTS

INTRODUCTION BY ERIC ZWEIG

"Sports is the toy department of life."

LEGENDARY SPORTSWRITER JIMMY CANNON

Although he still ranks among the greatest sportswriters ever, Jimmy Cannon has been dead since 1973. A lot has changed since then. For one thing, it's a little harder to think of sports as simply fun and games when so many of the athletes we're watching earn tens of millions of dollars. These days, with salary caps and labor disputes, sports news often winds up on the business page. And with the various other "distractions" of modern life, it too often becomes fodder for supermarket tabloids. But when it's played at its best, sports can still move us like few other things in life. It can move us to laughter. To tears. And right out of our seats with excitement!

There's a reason why Super Bowl XLIV (44, for those who aren't up on their Roman numerals) became the most-watched television program in American history in 2010, drawing an average audience of 106.5 million people in the United States. Yes, ratings systems have changed, but it was more than that. The victory of the New Orleans Saints was the ultimate feel-good, underdog story. Anyone who saw that Monday night game back in September of 2006, when the Saints returned to New Orleans after the devastation of Hurricane Katrina, saw how much sports can mean to a city. Their Super Bowl victory in 2010 was further proof of that. "New Orleans is back," exclaimed Saints owner Tom Benson, the Vince Lombardi Trophy held above his head, "and this shows the whole world. It's back!"

"We knew that we had an entire city, maybe an entire country behind us," said Saints quarterback Drew Brees. "I've been trying to imagine what this moment would be like for a long time. It's even better than expected."

Less than a week after the Super Bowl, the 2010 Winter Olympics opened in Vancouver, British Columbia. An average of 13.3 million Canadians watched every minute of the opening ceremonies. Overall, there were about 25 million Canadians who tuned in to some part of the festivities. While these numbers hardly approach the 106.5 million Americans of the Super Bowl audience, remember that Canada has a total population of less than 35 million people. That means that at some point, more than two out of every three Canadians was watching! A stunning 84 percent of all Canadians who had their TVs on that evening chose to watch the opening ceremonies. As *Toronto Star* media columnist Chris Zelkovich cracked, "it makes one wonder what the other 16 percent were looking at."

When Canada faced the United States in hockey to close out the preliminary round, the ratings averaged over 15 million people. When they met again in a gold medal rematch on the final day of competition, an average of 16.6 million Canadians were watching. There were 22 million tuned in to see Sidney Crosby score the game-winner in overtime.

When I get to visit classrooms and speak to children about the books I write, they often ask me why I became such a big sports fan. There's no one answer I can give them. Both my parents were sports fans. That certainly helped. Watching Paul Henderson score the winning goal in the 1972 Canada–Russia series on a TV in my classroom when I was only eight years old helped too. Playing organized sports as a boy was part of it, but so was the opportunity to ride my bike to the park and get together with friends on the weekend to play baseball and football games we organized ourselves. Too few kids, I think, get that opportunity these days. And yet, I hope the exploits of Sidney Crosby, the courage of figure skater Joannie Rochette, and the sheer exuberance of gravity-defying snowboarder Shaun White still inspire today's children the way the heroes of my youth helped inspire me.

Flipping through the pages of this book probably won't convince you to call your friends and get a game together, but I hope it will remind you of what you love about sports. The excitement, the drama and, sometimes, just the sheer absurdity of it. Yes, it's big business to the owners and the athletes, but for the rest of us, it's still fun and games!

So enjoy.

"**Somebody once asked me if I ever went up to the plate trying to hit a home run.** I said, 'Sure, everytime."

MICKEY MANTLE

Mickey Mantle

"You gotta be a man to play baseball for a living, but you gotta have a lot of little boy in you, too."

BROOKLYN DODGERS HALL OF FAME CATCHER ROY CAMPANELLA

"Age is a question of mind over matter.
If you don't mind, it doesn't matter."

NEGRO LEAGUE SUPERSTAR SATCHEL PAIGE, WHOSE TRUE AGE WAS UNKNOWN,
BUT WHO WAS THOUGHT TO BE 42 WHEN HE MADE HIS MAJOR LEAGUE DEBUT IN 1948

"Any ballplayer that don't sign autographs for little kids ain't an American. He's a communist."

RETIRED HALL OF FAMER ROGERS HORNSBY IN 1963

"How can anyone as slow as you pull a muscle?"

CINCINNATI RED PETE ROSE TO HIS TEAMMATE TONY PEREZ

"A good base stealer should make the whole infield jumpy. Whether you steal or not, you're changing the rhythm of the game. If the pitcher is concerned about you, he isn't concentrating enough on the batter."

HALL OF FAME SPEEDSTER-TURNED-BROADCASTER JOE MORGAN

"He looks like a greyhound, but he runs like a bus."

KANSAS CITY ROYAL GEORGE BRETT, ON TEAMMATE JAMIE QUIRK

"Trying to sneak a pitch past Hank Aaron is like trying to sneak the sunrise past a rooster."

MILWAUKEE BRAVES TEAMMATE JOE ADCOCK

"There have been only two geniuses in the world: Willie Mays and Willie Shakespeare."

ACTRESS AND BASEBALL FAN TALLULAH BANKHEAD

"He's got power enough to hit home runs in any park, including Yellowstone."

CINCINNATI REDS MANAGER SPARKY ANDERSON, ON PITTSBURGH PIRATES SLUGGER WILLIE STARGELL

"If somebody came up and hit .450, stole 100 bases and performed a miracle in the field every day, I'd still look you in the eye and say Willie Mays was better."

LEO DUROCHER, WHO MANAGED WILLIE MAYS IN HIS EARLY DAYS WITH THE NEW YORK GIANTS

"Like I say, it's almost embarrassing to talk about. I don't know if Michael Jordan or Bill Gates or Alexander the Great or anyone is worth this type of money, but that's the market we're in today. That's what Mr. Hicks decided to pay me, and now it's time to pay him back and win a couple championships."

ALEX RODRIGUEZ, AFTER SIGNING HIS 10-YEAR, $250-MILLION CONTRACT WITH THE TEXAS RANGERS

"The bigger the contract, the bigger the responsibility."

PEDRO MARTINEZ, ON SIGNING A DEAL WORTH $53 MILLION OVER FOUR YEARS
WITH THE NEW YORK METS AFTER THE 2004 SEASON

"Baseball has prostituted itself. Pretty soon we'll be starting games at midnight so the people in outer space can watch on prime time. We're making a mistake by always going for more money."

SAN DIEGO PADRES OWNER RAY KROC, ON TELEVISION'S CONTROL OF BASEBALL IN 1977

"They know when to cheer and they know when to boo. And they know when to drink beer. They do it all the time."

BREWERS SLUGGER GORMAN THOMAS ON THE FANS IN MILWAUKEE

"I don't care who you are, you hear those boos."

NEW YORK YANKEES LEGEND MICKEY MANTLE

"Catching is much like managing. Managers don't really win games, but they can lose plenty of them. The same way with catching."

PHILADELPHIA PHILLY BOB BOONE, WHO CAUGHT MORE MAJOR LEAGUE GAMES THAN ANYONE IN BASEBALL HISTORY

"That isn't an arm, that's a rifle."

FELLOW CATCHER GENE TENACE OF THE OAKLAND A'S
AFTER SEEING JOHNNY BENCH THROW TO SECOND BASE

"As a ballplayer, I would be delighted to do it again. As an individual, I doubt if I could possibly go through it again."

ROGER MARIS, ON HITTING 61 HOMERS IN 1961

"If I was going to storm a pillbox, going to sheer, utter, certain death, and the colonel said, 'Shepherd, pick six guys,' I'd pick six White Sox fans, because they have known death every day of their lives and it holds no terror for them."

HUMORIST JEAN SHEPHERD

"There's a fly ball to center field. Winfield is going back, back … He hits his head against the wall … It's rolling towards second base …"

JERRY COLEMAN

"So, like, what took you so long?"

PRESIDENT GEORGE W. BUSH, GREETING THE RED SOX AT THE WHITE HOUSE IN 2004

"It's not that Reggie is a bad outfielder. He just has trouble judging the ball and picking it up."

NEW YORK YANKEES MANAGER BILLY MARTIN, ON REGGIE JACKSON

"A hot dog at the ballpark is better than steak at the Ritz."

HUMPHREY BOGART

15

"All I want out of life is that when I walk down the street, folks will say, 'There goes the greatest hitter who ever lived.'"

"If I'd just tried for them dinky singles I could've batted around .600."

"I won more games than you ever saw."

"It starts out like a baseball, and when it gets to the plate it looks like a marble."

"I'm getting by on three pitches now – a curve, a change-up, and whatever you want to call that thing that used to be my fastball."

"You can't hit what you can't see."

"**Things were so bad in Chicago** last summer that by the **fifth inning** we were selling **hot dogs to go.**"

CHICAGO WHITE SOX PITCHER KEN BRETT

"Heck, if anybody told me I was setting a record I'd of got me some more strikeouts."

DIZZY DEAN, ON HIS NATIONAL LEAGUE RECORD 17 STRIKEOUTS ON JULY 30, 1933

"Son, what kind of a pitch would you like to miss?"

WHAT **DIZZY DEAN** IS SAID TO HAVE ASKED A BATTER HE HAD STRUCK OUT ALL DAY

"It ain't bragging if you can do it."

DIZZY DEAN

"Sure, old Diz knows the King's English. And not only that, I also know the Queen is English."

DIZZY DEAN, IN RESPONSE TO A LISTENER'S CLAIM THAT HE DIDN'T KNOW "THE KING'S ENGLISH"

"The runners have returned to their respectable bases."

A STANDARD **DIZZY DEAN** LINE

"One day I was pitching against Washington and the catcher called for a fastball. When it got to the plate, it was so slow that two pigeons were roosting on it. I decided to quit."

LONGTIME DETROIT TIGERS PITCHER PAUL "DIZZY" TROUT,
ON HOW HE KNEW IT WAS TIME TO RETIRE

"Being on the mound for that first pitch, it was like I actually existed."

TORONTO BLUE JAYS PITCHER DAVID BUSH, ON MAKING HIS MAJOR LEAGUE DEBUT IN 2004

"Ninety percent I'll spend on good times, women and Irish whiskey. The other ten percent I'll probably waste."

PHILADELPHIA PHILLIES RELIEVER TUG MCGRAW, ON HOW HE PLANNED TO SPEND HIS SALARY

"With the money I'm making, I should be playing two positions."

PHILADELPHIA PHILLY PETE ROSE, AFTER SIGNING WITH THE TEAM AS A FREE AGENT

"One year, I hit .291 and had to take a salary cut. If you hit .291 today, you'd own the franchise."

RETIRED HALL OF FAMER ENOS SLAUGHTER

"I got a million dollars worth of free advice, and a very small raise."

BROOKLYN DODGER EDDIE STANKY, ON NEGOTIATING WITH BRANCH RICKEY

"I don't recall the name, but you sure were a sucker for a high curve inside."

"It's not easy to hit .215. You have to be going terrible and have bad luck, too."

STRUGGLING PITTSBURGH PIRATES OUTFIELDER STEVE KEMP

"The only mistake I made in my whole baseball career was hitting .361 that one year, because ever since then people have expected me to keep on doing it."

DETROIT TIGER AND 1961 AMERICAN LEAGUE BATTING CHAMPION NORM CASH

"I can't very well tell my batters, 'Don't hit it to him.' Wherever they hit it, he's there anyway."

NEW YORK METS MANAGER GIL HODGES, ON WILLIE MAYS

"He can play all three outfield positions — at the same time."

LONG-TIME MANAGER GENE MAUCH, ON CESAR CEDENO OF THE HOUSTON ASTROS

"He has muscles in his hair."

LEFTY GOMEZ, ON HALL OF FAME SLUGGER JIMMIE FOXX

"When I hit a ball, I want someone else to go chase it."

.358 LIFETIME HITTER ROGERS HORNSBY, ON GOLF

"I don't want them to forget Ruth. I just want them to remember me."

"When Neil Armstrong set foot on the moon, all the scientists were puzzled by an unidentifiable white object. I knew immediately what it was. That was a home run ball hit off me in 1937 by Jimmy Foxx."

LEFTY GOMEZ

"I was so bad I never even broke a bat until last year. Then I was backing out of the garage."

LEFTY GOMEZ, A NOTORIOUSLY POOR-HITTING PITCHER, ON HIS LACK OF BATTING SKILL

"One of my chores was to milk the cows, which meant getting up before dawn and going out to that cold, dark barn. I didn't expect to make it all the way to the big leagues; I just had to get away from them damn cows."

CINCINNATI REDS HALL OF FAME OUTFIELDER EDD ROUSH (1913 TO 1931),
ON WHY HE GOT INTO BASEBALL

"I got a jackass back in Oklahoma. You can work him from sunup till sundown, and he ain't never gonna win the Kentucky Derby."

ST. LOUIS CARDINAL PEPPER MARTIN,
WHEN ASKED BY A COACH TO WORK TWICE AS HARD IN PRACTICE

"A pitcher has to look at the hitter as his mortal enemy."

CLEVELAND INDIANS HALL OF FAME PITCHER EARLY WYNN

"The pitcher has got only a ball. I've got a bat. So the percentage in weapons is in my favor and I let the fellow with the ball do the fretting."

HALL OF FAMER AND HOME RUN KING **HANK AARON**

"I don't want to give all my little things out. Hitters are pretty stupid, but they do read the papers."

NEW YORK YANKEES PITCHER **RANDY JOHNSON**,
DISCUSSING HIS SLIDER WITH NEW YORK TIMES WRITER TYLER KEPNER

"Baseball is the only sport I know that when you're on offense, the other team controls the ball."

FORMER MAJOR LEAGUER **KEN (HAWK) HARRELSON**

"When you play this game 20 years, go to bat 10,000 times, and get 3,000 hits, do you know what that means? You've gone 0 for 7,000."

BASEBALL'S ALL-TIME HIT LEADER **PETE ROSE**, WHO HAD 4,256 HITS IN 14,053 AT-BATS

"We tell him, 'Hey, slow down. After you touch home plate there is no other base to run to.'"

LOS ANGELES DODGER **RICK MONDAY** ON TEAMMATE STEVE SAX

"This guy is so old that the first time he had athlete's foot, he used Absorbine Sr."

BROADCASTER **BOB COSTAS**, ON 45-YEAR-OLD PITCHER TOMMY JOHN

"Greg Maddux could put a baseball through a life saver if you asked him."

HALL OF FAME PLAYER-TURNED-BROADCASTER JOE MORGAN

"Correct thinkers think that 'baseball trivia' is an oxymoron: nothing about baseball is trivial."

GEORGE WILL, POLITICAL COMMENTATOR AND AUTHOR OF THE BASEBALL BOOK MEN AT WORK

"Bob Gibson is the luckiest pitcher I ever saw. He always pitches when the other team doesn't score any runs."

ST. LOUIS CARDINALS CATCHER TIM MCCARVER, ON BATTERYMATE BOB GIBSON, WHO WAS 22-9 WITH A 1.12 ERA IN 1968

"I'm a terrible singer. I feel lucky to play baseball. You can't be gifted in everything."

SEATTLE MARINER ALEX RODRIGUEZ

"There are only two kinds of managers: winning managers and ex-managers."

GIL HODGES, MANAGER OF THE 1969 "MIRACLE METS"

"I'm not the manager because I'm always right, but I'm always right because I'm the manager."

MONTREAL EXPOS MANAGER GENE MAUCH

"The toughest thing for me as a young manager is that a lot of my players saw me play. They know how bad I was."

CHICAGO WHITE SOX MANAGER TONY LARUSSA

"I'm happy for him, that is, if you think becoming a big-league manager is a good thing to have happen to you."

LEGENDARY DODGERS MANAGER WALTER ALSTON, ON LEARNING THAT FORMER DODGERS PLAYER GIL HODGES HAD BEEN NAMED MANAGER OF THE NEW YORK METS

"I never took the game home with me. I always left it in some bar."

BOB LEMON, A HALL OF FAME PITCHER WHO MANAGED THE ROYALS, WHITE SOX AND YANKEES BETWEEN 1970 AND 1982

"I wish I was half the ballplayer he is."

DETROIT TIGERS HALL OF FAMER AL KALINE, ON MICKEY MANTLE

"I always loved the game, but when my legs weren't hurting it was a lot easier to love."

MICKEY MANTLE, ON HIS MANY INJURIES

"If he was throwing the ball any better, we'd have to start a new league for him."

UMPIRE JOHN KIBLER, ON DWIGHT GOODEN DURING HIS SENSATIONAL 1984 ROOKIE SEASON WITH THE NEW YORK METS

"I threw so hard I thought my arm would fly right off my body."

BOSTON RED SOX PITCHER SMOKEY JOE WOOD, AFTER BEATING THE NEW YORK GIANTS IN GAME ONE OF THE 1912 WORLD SERIES

"Blind people come to the park just to listen to him pitch."

HALL OF FAME SLUGGER **REGGIE JACKSON** ON HALL OF FAME PITCHER TOM SEAVER

"Fans don't boo nobodies."

REGGIE JACKSON, WHILE A MEMBER OF THE OAKLAND A'S

"Why certainly I'd like to have that fellow who hits a home run every time at bat, who strikes out every opposing batter when he's pitching, who throws strikes to any base or the plate when he's playing outfield and who's always thinking about two innings ahead just what he'll do to baffle the other team. Any manager would want a guy like that playing for him. The only trouble is to get him to put down his cup of beer and come down out of the stands and do those things."

PITTSBURGH PIRATES MANAGER **DANNY MURTAUGH**

"I didn't come to New York to be a star. I brought my star with me."

REGGIE JACKSON, ON SIGNING WITH THE YANKEES IN 1977

"Trying to hit him was like trying to drink coffee with a fork."

PITTSBURGH PIRATES HALL OF FAME SLUGGER **WILLIE STARGELL**, ON FACING LOS ANGELES DODGERS STAR SANDY KOUFAX

"He must have made that before he died."

NEW YORK YANKEES HALL OF FAMER **YOGI BERRA**, AFTER SEEING A STEVE MCQUEEN MOVIE

"A good friend of mine used to say, 'This is a very simple game. You throw the ball, you catch the ball, you hit the ball. Sometimes you win, sometimes you lose, some times it rains.' Think about that for a while."

NUKE LALOOSH (TIM ROBBINS), IN THE MOVIE BULL DURHAM

"It's supposed to be hard! If it wasn't hard, everyone would do it. The hard is what makes it great!"

JIMMY DUGAN (TOM HANKS), TO DOTTIE HINSON (GEENA DAVIS), ON BEING A BASEBALL PLAYER IN THE MOVIE A LEAGUE OF THEIR OWN

"He had an ERA of 3.84 and an IQ to match."

JIM BOUTON, AUTHOR OF THE BASEBALL TELL-ALL BOOK BALL FOUR, ON A FELLOW PITCHER

"I get tired of hearing my ballplayers bellyache all the time. They should sit in the pressbox sometimes and watch themselves play."

SAN DIEGO PADRES PRESIDENT BUZZIE BAVASI

"It will revolutionize baseball. It will open a whole new area of alibis for the players."

LONGTIME BASEBALL EXECUTIVE GABE PAUL, ON ARTIFICIAL TURF

"Do you know what the cardinal sin was on that ball club? To begin a sentence to McGraw with the words 'I thought ...' 'You thought?' he would yell. 'With what?'"

HALL OF FAMER FREDDIE LINSTROM,
ON LEGENDARY NEW YORK GIANTS MANAGER JOHN MCGRAW

"He can run, hit, throw and field. The only thing Willie Davis has never been able to do is think."

CALIFORNIA ANGELS GENERAL MANAGER BUZZIE BAVASI

"It'll be great not to have to listen to two national anthems."

OUTFIELDER MITCH WEBSTER, ON BEING TRADED TO THE CHICAGO CUBS
AFTER PLAYING FOR THE TORONTO BLUE JAYS AND THE MONTREAL EXPOS

"There are three types of baseball players: those who make it happen, those who watch it happen, and those who wonder what happened."

LOS ANGELES DODGERS MANAGER TOMMY LASORDA

"My only day off is the day I pitch."

ROGER CLEMENS,
ON HIS LEGENDARY WORKOUT ROUTINE

"I once loved this game. But after being traded four times, I realized that it's nothing but a business. I treat my horses better than the owners treat us."

SLUGGER AND FREE SPIRIT DICK ALLEN, WHO PLAYED ON FIVE DIFFERENT TEAMS IN A 15-YEAR CAREER

"A man once told me to walk with the Lord. I'd rather walk with the bases loaded."

BALTIMORE ORIOLE KEN SINGLETON

"You know Earl. He's not happy unless he's not happy."

BALTIMORE ORIOLES PLAYER AND COACH ELROD HENDRICKS ON ORIOLES MANAGER EARL WEAVER

"Good pitching will always stop good hitting and vice versa."

NEW YORK YANKEES HALL OF FAME MANAGER CASEY STENGEL

"He has the personality of a tree trunk."

NEW YORK METS CATCHER JOHN STEARNS, ON TEAMMATE DAVE KINGMAN

"He's not moody, he's just mean. When you're moody, you're sometimes nice."

NEW YORK YANKEES RELIEVER SPARKY LYLE, ON YANKEES CATCHER THURMAN MUNSON

"It takes him an hour and a half to watch "60 Minutes"."

HOUSTON ASTROS EXECUTIVE DONALD DAVIDSON ON ASTRO JOE NIEKRO'S ABILITY TO RELAX

"I'm not sure I know what the hell charisma is, but I get the feeling it's Willie Mays."

CINCINNATI REDS FIRST BASEMAN TED KLUSZEWSKI

"There is one word in America that says it all, and that one word is 'you never know.'"

PITCHER JOAQUIN ANDUJAR, WHO TWICE WON 20 GAMES FOR THE ST. LOUIS CARDINALS

"Trade a player a year too early rather than a year too late."

LEGENDARY BASEBALL EXECUTIVE BRANCH RICKEY, LONGTIME GENERAL MANAGER
OF THE ST. LOUIS CARDINALS, BROOKLYN DODGERS AND PITTSBURGH PIRATES,
AND THE MAN WHO BROUGHT JACKIE ROBINSON TO THE MAJOR LEAGUES

"You gotta be careful with your body. Your body is like a bar of soap. The more you use it, the more it wears down."

DICK ALLEN, WHO WAS TRADED FIVE TIMES IN HIS 15-YEAR CAREER

"Close doesn't count in baseball. Close only counts in horseshoes and grenades."

HALL OF FAME SLUGGER FRANK ROBINSON, WHO BECAME THE FIRST BLACK MANAGER
IN BASEBALL HISTORY WITH THE CLEVELAND INDIANS IN 1975

"Baseball stuck. Sunday school didn't."

GEORGE WILL, POLITICAL COMMENTATOR AND AUTHOR OF THE BASEBALL BOOK MEN AT WORK

"Touch 'em all Joe. You'll never hit a bigger home run in your life!"

TORONTO BLUE JAYS BROADCASTER TOM CHEEK,
CALLING JOE CARTER'S THREE-RUN HOMER IN THE BOTTOM OF THE NINTH
THAT DEFEATED THE PHILADELPHIA PHILLIES IN THE 1993 WORLD SERIES

"Pitching is really just an internal struggle between the pitcher and his stuff. If my curve ball is breaking and I'm throwing it where I want, the batter is irrelevant."

BALTIMORE ORIOLES PITCHER STEVE STONE, 1980 AMERICAN LEAGUE CY YOUNG AWARD WINNER

"It's the greatest thing in the world when you're a pitcher and you get a hitter looking for one pitch and you throw the other pitch. And you know he was looking for the other pitch, because he never took the bat off his shoulder and it was right down the middle."

NEW YORK YANKEES PITCHER RANDY JOHNSON

"The dumber a pitcher is, the better. When he gets smart and begins to experiment with a lot of different pitches, he's in trouble. All I ever had was a fastball, a curve and a change-up and I did pretty good."

ST. LOUIS CARDINALS HALL OF FAMER DIZZY DEAN

"I could probably throw harder if I wanted, but why? When they're in a jam, a lot of pitchers ... try to throw harder. Me, I try to locate better."

ATLANTA BRAVES PITCHER GREG MADDUX

"It's a great day for a ballgame; let's play two."

SIGNATURE LINE OF CHICAGO CUBS HALL OF FAMER ERNIE BANKS

"It's not what you did last year. It's what you're going to do this year. That's more important."

ST. LOUIS CARDINALS SLUGGER ALBERT PUJOLS

"The best thing about baseball is that you can do something about yesterday tomorrow."

PHILADELPHIA PHILLIES INFIELDER MANNY TRILLO

"When I was a small boy in Kansas, a friend of mine and I went fishing and as we sat there in the warmth of the summer afternoon on a river bank, we talked about what we wanted to do when we grew up. I told him I wanted to be a real major league baseball player. ... My friend said that he'd like to be president of the United States. Neither of us got our wish."

PRESIDENT DWIGHT D. EISENHOWER

"I throw the ball right down the middle. The high-ball hitters swing over it and the low-ball hitters swing under it."

PITCHER SAUL ROGOVIN, WHO HAD A 48-48 RECORD WITH FOUR DIFFERENT CLUBS DURING HIS EIGHT-YEAR CAREER

"I know, but I had a better year than Hoover."

NEW YORK YANKEES STAR BABE RUTH, WHOSE $80,000 SALARY IN 1931 WAS MORE THAN THE $75,000 EARNED BY PRESIDENT HERBERT HOOVER

Most ball games
are lost, not won.

CASEY STENGEL

"He's dead at the present time."

CASEY STENGEL, REFERRING TO BOSTON BRAVES OUTFIELDER LARRY GILBERT, WHO HAD DIED THE YEAR BEFORE

"Best thing wrong with Jack Fisher is nothing."

CASEY STENGEL, ON HIS TOP PITCHER WHEN HE WAS MANAGING THE NEW YORK METS

"How the hell should I know? Most of the people my age are dead."

CASEY STENGEL, WHEN ASKED WHAT MOST PEOPLE "YOUR AGE" THINK ABOUT MODERN-DAY BASEBALL

"Mister, that boy couldn't hit the ground if he fell out of an airplane."

CASEY STENGEL, ON A PROSPECT HE SENT TO THE MINORS

"Oldtimers' weekends and airplane landings are alike. If you can walk away from them, they're successful."

CASEY STENGEL

"This is really more fun than being president. I really do love baseball and I wish we could do this out on the lawn every day. I wouldn't even complain if a stray ball came through the Oval Office window now and then."

PRESIDENT RONALD REAGAN, ON PLAYING BASEBALL WITH OLDTIMERS WHILE CELEBRATING NATIONAL BASEBALL MONTH IN 1983

"Hot as Hell, ain't it, Prez?"

BABE RUTH, ON BEING INTRODUCED TO PRESIDENT CALVIN COOLIDGE
ON A WARM DAY AT THE BALLPARK IN WASHINGTON

"I have the greatest job in the world. Only one person can have it. You have shortstops on other teams — I'm not knocking other teams — but there's only one shortstop on the Yankees."

NEW YORK YANKEE DEREK JETER

"It's great to be young and a Yankee."

HALL OF FAMER WAITE HOYT, WHO PITCHED WITH THE YANKEES FROM 1921 TO 1930

"I think the good Lord is a Yankee."

NEW YORK YANKEES RELIEF ACE MARIANO RIVERA

"To play 18 years in Yankee Stadium is the best thing that could ever happen to a ballplayer."

NEW YORK YANKEES GREAT MICKEY MANTLE

"His reputation preceded him before he got here."

NEW YORK YANKEES SLUGGER DON MATTINGLY, ON FACING THE METS' DWIGHT GOODEN
IN AN EXHIBITION GAME

"Man, it was tough.
The wind was blowing about 100 degrees."

TEXAS RANGER MICKEY RIVERS

"Well, that was a cliff-dweller."

NEW YORK METS MANAGER WES WESTRUM, AFTER A CLOSE GAME

"I called the doctor and he told me the contraptions were an hour apart."

NEW YORK METS CATCHER MACKEY SASSER, ON HOW HE KNEW HIS WIFE HAD GONE INTO LABOR

"It's not a question of morality."

PHILADELPHIA PHILLIES MANAGER DANNY OZARK, WHEN ASKED ABOUT HIS TEAM'S MORALE

"O.K., now, everyone inhale and ... dehale."

LOS ANGELES DODGERS SHORTSTOP MAURY WILLS, LEADING THE TEAM
THROUGH CALISTHENICS IN 1962

"Whenever I've pitched, it's been a Samson and Goliath story."

SIX-FOOT-TEN INCH NEW YORK YANKEES RANDY JOHNSON, MIXING UP BIBLE STORIES

"Me and George and Billy are two of a kind."

MICKEY RIVERS, DENYING HE'D HAVE TROUBLE WITH GEORGE STEINBRENNER
AND BILLY MARTIN IF HE RETURNED TO THE NEW YORK YANKEES

"Any **ballplayer** that don't sign **autographs** for little kids ain't an **American**. He's a **communist**."

RETIRED HALL OF FAMER ROGER HORNSBY IN 1963

"Right now, I feel like I've got my feet on the ground as far as my head is concerned."

SAM BOWEN, A 1974 BOSTON RED SOX DRAFT PICK

"I knew I was going to take the wrong train, so I left early."

YOGI BERRA

"You don't want to be a loser and a winner at the same time, I guess."

SAN DIEGO CATCHER ROBERT FICK ON THE POSSIBILITY OF THE 2005 PADRES
WINNING THE NL WEST WITH A RECORD BELOW .500

"They're coming out in groves."

BABE RUTH

"You can pitch a gem and lose, but you can't lose when you win."

SAN DIEGO PADRES PITCHER ERIC SHOW

"This is the latest I've ever seen nothing not happen."

TORONTO BLUE JAYS GM J.P. RICCARDI ON THE LACK OF DEALS BEING MADE
AS THE 2005 TRADE DEADLINE APPROACHED

"It's a beautiful day for a night game."

BROADCASTER AND FORMER MANAGER AND HALL OF FAME PLAYER FRANKIE FRISCH

"That's the true harbinger of spring, not crocuses or swallows returning to Capistrano, but the sound of a bat on the ball."

BILL VEECK, WHILE OWNER OF THE CHICAGO WHITE SOX IN 1976

"These days baseball is different. You come to spring training, you get your legs ready, your arms loose, your agents ready, your lawyer lined up."

HALL OF FAMER DAVE WINFIELD (WHO PLAYED FOR SIX TEAMS IN HIS 22-YEAR CAREER) ON BASEBALL IN THE FREE AGENT ERA

"Baseball is dull only to dull minds."

LEGENDARY SPORTSWRITER RED SMITH

"There is still nothing in life as constant and as changing at the same time as an afternoon at a ballpark."

TV PERSONALITY AND COLUMNIST LARRY KING

"I can never understand why anybody leaves the game early to beat the traffic. The purpose of baseball is to keep you from caring if you beat the traffic."

KANSAS CITY STAR COLUMNIST BILL VAUGHAN

"When you're hitting the ball, it comes at you looking like a grapefruit. When you're not, it looks like a black-eyed pea."

BOSTON RED SOX SLUGGER GEORGE SCOTT, WHO HIT .268 WTH 271 HOMERS OVER A 14-YEAR CAREER

> "Just take the ball and throw [it] where you want to. **Throw strikes.** Home plate don't move."
>
> SATCHEL PAIGE

"Baseball's most delicious paradox: although the game never changes, you've never seen everything."

NEW ENGLAND HORRORMEISTER STEPHEN KING,
WRITING IN THE 2004 RED SOX CHRONICLE FAITHFUL

"I have always maintained that the best remedy for a batting slump is two wads of cotton. One in each ear."

MAVERICK BASEBALL OWNER BILL VEECK, WHO RAN THE CLEVELAND INDIANS,
ST. LOUIS BROWNS AND CHICAGO WHITE SOX BETWEEN 1946 AND 1980

"Was it difficult to leave the Titanic?"

SAL BANDO, ON HIS DECISION TO LEAVE THE SUCCESSFUL BUT SQUABBLING OAKLAND A'S

"No, why should I?"

NEW YORK YANKEES PITCHER DON LARSEN, WHEN ASKED IF HE EVER GOT TIRED OF SPEAKING
ABOUT HIS PERFECT GAME IN THE 1956 WORLD SERIES

"I've got to. I can't dance or sing, and we've already got a pitching coach."

LOS ANGELES DODGERS PITCHER DON SUTTON, WHEN TOLD TO "HANG IN THERE"
BY MANAGER TOMMY LASORDA

"Hey big mouth, how do you spell triple?"

INFAMOUS CHICAGO WHITE SOX STAR SHOELESS JOE JACKSON,
AFTER HITTING A THREE-BAGGER, TO A HECKLING FAN WHO KEPT ASKING
IF HE COULD SPELL ILLITERATE

"It has to be physical. That's why I'm soaking my arm now. If it was mental, I'd be soaking my head."

BOSTON RED SOX PITCHER **JIM LONBORG**, WHO PITCHED ON ONLY TWO DAYS REST
IN THE 1967 WORLD SERIES, WHEN ASKED IF THE DIFFICULTIES WERE MORE PHYSICAL OR MENTAL

"Why, Mr. Summers, don't you know that the spitter has been outlawed for years? How would I ever learn to throw one?"

DETROIT TIGERS PITCHER **TOMMY BRIDGES** TO UMPIRE BILL SUMMERS
AFTER BEING ACCUSED OF THROWING A SPITBALL

"I'd always have [grease] in at least two places, in case the umpires would ask me to wipe off one. I never wanted to be caught out here without anything. It wouldn't be professional."

HALL OF FAME PITCHER, AND NOTED SPITBALLER, **GAYLORD PERRY**

"We used to walk up and down the dugout saying, 'Forget about it, hit the dry side.' He'd throw it twice and you'd be looking for it on 116 pitches."

BALTIMORE ORIOLES MANAGER **EARL WEAVER** ON FACING GAYLORD PERRY

"It didn't hurt or help me. I just didn't want to take any chances."

PITTSBURGH PIRATES HALL OF FAMER AND SEVEN-TIME NATIONAL LEAGUE HOME RUN CHAMPION
RALPH KINER, WHO NEVER STEPPED ON THE FOUL LINE

"You can't think and hit at the same time."
YOGI BERRA

"A nickel ain't worth a dime anymore."
YOGI BERRA

"So I'm ugly. So what? I never saw anyone hit with his face."
YOGI BERRA

"If the people don't want to come out to the park, nobody's going to stop them."
YOGI BERRA, ON ATTENDANCE WOES IN KANSAS CITY

"It's so crowded nobody goes there anymore."
YOGI BERRA, ON TOOTS SHOR'S RESTAURANT

"Willie Mays, Hank Aaron, myself, the home run hitters of my time, we were considered big. Now, we'd be midgets."

WASHINGTON NATIONALS MANAGER FRANK ROBINSON, WHO WAS SIX-FOOT-ONE
AND 195 POUNDS IN HIS PLAYING DAYS AND HIT 586 HOME RUNS

"Good news. Ten awards have been given out so far, and not one winner has tested positive for steroids."

COMEDIAN CHRIS ROCK, TAKING A SHOT AT BASEBALL
WHILE HOSTING THE 2005 ACADEMY AWARDS

"Superstitious people don't discuss their superstitions."

RUSTY STAUB, WHO PLAYED 23 MAJOR LEAGUE SEASONS FOR FIVE DIFFERENT TEAMS
(INCLUDING THE NEW YORK METS AND MONTREAL EXPOS TWICE) FROM 1963 TO 1985

"I never took steroids, because I don't need them. The stuff I take, I buy over the counter."

TAMPA BAY DEVIL RAY ALEX SANCHEZ, ADMITTING HE USES MULTIVITAMINS
AND ENERGY-BOOSTING MILKSHAKES BUT DENYING HE USES STEROIDS,
AFTER BECOMING THE FIRST PLAYER TO FAIL MAJOR LEAGUE BASEBALL'S TEST
FOR PERFORMANCE-ENHANCING SUBSTANCES

"Not intentionally, but I sweat easy."

NEW YORK YANKEES HALL OF FAMER LEFTY GOMEZ, WHEN ASKED IF HE THREW A SPITBALL

"Just one. Whenever I hit a home run, I make certain I touch all four bases."

NEW YORK YANKEES STAR BABE RUTH, ON SUPERSTITIONS

"I feel my ability as a ballplayer is overshadowed by people saying, 'Hey, look at that idiot at the plate.'"

CLEVELAND INDIAN **MIKE HARGROVE**, WHO WAS NICKNAMED "THE HUMAN RAIN DELAY"
FOR HIS IDIOSYNCRATIC MANEUVERS BEFORE STEPPING INTO THE BATTER'S BOX

"This losing streak is bad for the fans, no doubt, but look at it this way. We're making a lot of people happy in other cities."

ATLANTA BRAVES OWNER **TED TURNER** FINDS A SILVER LINING DURING A SLUMP

"Even Napoleon had his Watergate."

PHILADELPHIA PHILLIES MANAGER **DANNY OZARK**, AFTER A TEN-GAME LOSING STREAK

"Mostly bums."

HALL OF FAMER **ROGERS HORNSBY**, WHEN MANAGING THE BOSTON BRAVES
AND ASKED BY THE OWNER WHAT KIND OF TEAM HE HAD

"I've always swung the same way. The difference is when I swing and miss, people say, 'He's swinging for the fences.' But when I swing and make contact people say, 'That's a nice swing.' But there's no difference, it's the same swing."

CHICAGO CUBS SLUGGER **SAMMY SOSA**,
THE ONLY PLAYER IN HISTORY WITH THREE 60-HOMER SEASONS

"He **pitches** as though
he's **double parked.** "

LEGENDARY DODGERS ANNOUNCER VIN SCULLY, ON ST. LOUIS CARDINALS GREAT BOB GIBSON

"I swing as hard as I can, and I try to swing right through the ball. … The harder you grip the bat, the more you can swing it through the ball, and the farther the ball will go. I swing big, with everything I've got. I hit big or I miss big. I like to live as big as I can."

NEW YORK YANKEES SLUGGER BABE RUTH, WHO HIT 714 HOME RUNS

"I think of myself as 'catching' the ball with my bat and letting the pitcher supply the power."

SAN FRANCISCO GIANTS SLUGGER BARRY BONDS, JUST THE THIRD PLAYER IN HISTORY TO HIT OVER 700 HOME RUNS

"Hitting is 50 percent above the shoulders."

TED WILLIAMS, AS MANAGER OF THE WASHINGTON SENATORS. HE HIT .344 WITH 521 HOMERS DURING HIS CAREER WITH THE BOSTON RED SOX

"Hitting is an art, but not an exact science."

EIGHT-TIME AMERICAN LEAGUE BATTING CHAMP ROD CAREW, WHO HIT .328 IN A 19-YEAR CAREER WITH THE MINNESOTA TWINS AND CALIFORNIA ANGELS

"I don't think I can get into my deep inner thoughts about hitting. It's like talking about religion."

PHILADELPHIA PHILLIES HALL OF FAMER MIKE SCHMIDT, WHO LED THE NATIONAL LEAGUE IN HOMERS A RECORD EIGHT TIMES

"Keep your eye on the ball and hit 'em where they ain't."

WEE WILLIE KEELER, WHO HIT .424 FOR THE OLD BALTIMORE ORIOLES IN 1897

"Any umpire who claims he has never missed a play is ... well, an umpire."

UMPIRE RON LUCIANO

"It seems to me the official rule book should be called the funny pages. It obviously doesn't mean anything. The rule book is only good for you when you go deer hunting and run out of toilet paper."

NEW YORK YANKEES MANAGER BILLY MARTIN

"I never questioned the integrity of an umpire. Their eyesight, yes."

LEGENDARY MANAGER LEO DUROCHER

"Gentlemen, he was out because I said he was out."

HALL OF FAME UMPIRE BILL KLEM, AFTER BEING SHOWN PHOTOGRAPHIC EVIDENCE THAT HE HAD BLOWN A CALL

"Tests showed there was a brain."

NEW YORK YANKEES PITCHER CARL PAVANO, WHO WAS DIAGNOSED WITH A CONCUSSION AFTER TAKING A LINE DRIVE OFF HIS HEAD EARLY IN THE 2005 SEASON

"I'm throwing just as hard as I ever did. The ball's just not getting there as fast."

BOSTON RED SOX PITCHER LEFTY GROVE,
A FUTURE HALL OF FAMER, ON THE PROBLEMS OF AGING

"No more than usual."

"The doctors X-rayed my head and found nothing."

"It's like the Kennedy assassination. Everyone I see comes up and tells me where they were and what they were doing when Gibson hit that home run."

"Why pitch nine innings when you can get just as famous pitching two?"

"The two most important things in life are good friends and a strong bullpen."

"It's the best feeling in the world. The game's on the line, and you're the guy in the spotlight."

LOS ANGELES DODGERS CLOSER **ERIC GAGNE**

"I told him I wasn't tired. He told me, 'No, but the outfielders sure are.'"

TEXAS RANGERS RELIEVER **JIM KERN**, ON WHAT THE MANAGER SAID
WHEN TAKING HIM OUT OF A GAME

"He can't hit, he can't run, he can't field, he can't throw. He can't do a goddamn thing but beat you."

BROOKLYN DODGERS GM **BRANCH RICKEY** ON EDDIE STANKY

"My dad would have bopped me on the head when I was a kid if I came home bragging about what I did on the field. He only wanted to know what the team did."

KEN GRIFFEY, JR. ON HIS FATHER, KEN GRIFFEY, SR.

"And if I have my choice between a pennant and a triple crown, I'll take the pennant every time."

BOSTON RED SOX STAR **CARL YASTRZEMSKI**, WHO WON BOTH IN 1967

"The death toll in New England will be catastrophic.
There are so many old people saying,
   'I can't die until I see them win the World Series.'
They are all going to die.
   It's going to be worse than the Black Plague.

BOSTON RED SOX FAN PAUL SULLIVAN,
ON THE DOWNSIDE OF BOSTON WINNING THE 2004 WORLD SERIES

"If you're going to play at all, you're out to win. Baseball, board games, playing Jeopardy, I hate to lose."

NEW YORK YANKEES STAR **DEREK JETER**

"When you work for George Steinbrenner, whether you're the favorite or you're not the favorite, you're expected to win."

NEW YORK YANKEES MANAGER **JOE TORRE**

"Whoever answers the bullpen phone."

TEXAS RANGERS PITCHING COACH **CHUCK ESTRADA**, ON HOW HE DECIDES
WHICH RELIEVER TO USE ON HIS LAST-PLACE TEAM

"If I were playing third base and my mother were rounding third with the run that was going to beat us, I'd trip her. Oh, I'd pick her up and brush her off and say, 'Sorry, Mom,' but nobody beats me."

LEGENDARY MANAGER (AND SCRAPPY EX-PLAYER) **LEO DUROCHER**

"On my tombstone, just write: 'The sorest loser that ever lived.'"

BALTIMORE ORIOLES MANAGER **EARL WEAVER**

"I don't want to mellow. I'd rather be known as a winner and a poor loser."

BOSTON RED SOX MANAGER **DICK WILLIAMS**

"Grantland Rice, the great sportswriter, once said, 'It's not whether you win or lose, it's how you play the game.' Well Grantland Rice can go to hell, as far as I'm concerned."

LONGTIME CALIFORNIA ANGELS OWNER (AND FORMER SINGING COWBOY) **GENE AUTRY**

"You have to bear in mind that Mr. Autry's favorite horse was named Champion. He ain't ever had one called Runner-Up."

CALIFORNIA ANGELS MANAGER **GENE MAUCH**, ON THE CLUB OWNER

"We have deep depth."

NEW YORK YANKEES HALL OF FAME CATCHER **YOGI BERRA**

"Our similarities are different."

DALE BERRA, COMPARING HIMSELF TO HIS FAMOUS FATHER YOGI

"I don't know nothin' about nothin', I'm just glad we won."

BLUE JAYS PITCHER **JIM ACKER**, WHEN ASKED FOR HIS THOUGHTS
AFTER TORONTO WON THE AMERICAN LEAGUE EAST IN 1985

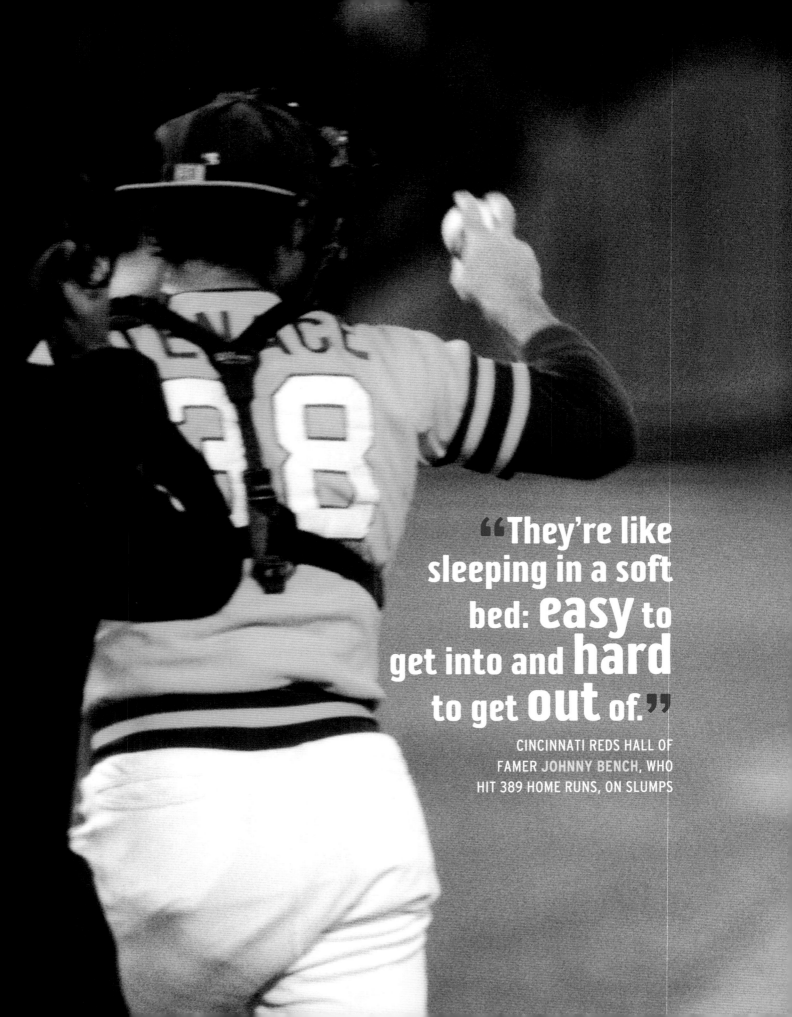

"They're like sleeping in a soft bed: easy to get into and hard to get out of."

CINCINNATI REDS HALL OF
FAMER JOHNNY BENCH, WHO
HIT 389 HOME RUNS, ON SLUMPS

There are three types of football players. First, there are those who are winners and know they are winners. Then there are the losers who know they're losers. Then there are those who aren't winners but don't know it. They're the ones for me. They never quit trying. They're the soul of our game.

UNIVERSITY OF ALABAMA FOOTBALL COACH

"Ability is what you're capable of doing. Motivation determines what you do. Attitude determines how well you do it."

COLLEGE FOOTBALL COACH LOU HOLTZ

"Football isn't necessarily won by the best players. It's won by the team with the best attitude."

WASHINGTON REDSKINS COACH GEORGE ALLEN

"One player was lost because he broke his nose. How do you go about getting a nose in condition for football?"

UNIVERSITY OF TEXAS FOOTBALL COACH DARRELL ROYAL, WHEN ASKED IF THE ABNORMAL
NUMBER OF LONGHORNS' INJURIES IN 1966 HAD RESULTED FROM POOR PHYSICAL CONDITIONING

"The only thing soft about Larry Csonka is his nose."

AUTHOR AL LEVINE, ON THE MIAMI DOLPHINS FULLBACK
WHO HAD BROKEN HIS NOSE ABOUT A DOZEN TIMES

"I wasn't much good. When I went into the line on a fake, I would holler, 'I don't have it.'"

COMEDIAN BOB NEWHART, ON HIS HIGH SCHOOL FOOTBALL CAREER

"They should put a sign on the 10-yard line saying THE BUCS STOP HERE."

BROADCASTER JACK HARRIS, ON TAMPA BAY'S WEAK OFFENSE
IN THE BUCCANEERS' EARLY YEARS

"It wasn't as easy as you think. It's hard to stay awake that long."

"No wonder you guys got kicked around. Every guy on the team has still got all his teeth."

"He said: 'Gosh, Dad, that means we're not going to any more bowl games.'"

"Running into him was like running into an electric shock."

"To me, Jack not only typified what a defensive end is, he also typified what a football player is. If a Martian landed in my backyard, knocked on my door and asked me, 'What's a football player?' I'd go get Jack Youngblood."

"Football doesn't build character.
It eliminates the weak ones."

UNIVERSITY OF TEXAS FOOTBALL COACH **DARRELL ROYAL**

"He doesn't know anything about drugs. He still thinks uppers are dentures."

FORMER OHIO STATE RUNNING BACK **ARCHIE GRIFFIN**, ON COACH WOODY HAYES

"When he goes on safari, the lions roll up their windows."

MIAMI DOLPHINS OFFENSIVE LINE COACH **MONTE CLARK**, ON FULLBACK LARRY CSONKA

"They didn't hesitate: Wendy's, McDonald's, Pizza Hut and Burger King."

DENVER BRONCOS TEAM NUTRITIONIST **JACKIE BERNING**,
AFTER ASKING PLAYERS TO NAME THE FOUR BASIC FOOD GROUPS

"When you hang with a bunch of 300-pound linemen, you tend to find the places that are the greasiest and serve the most food."

NEW ENGLAND PATRIOTS QUARTERBACK **TOM BRADY**, ON THE PLACES HE LIKES TO EAT

"I'm on a seafood diet. I eat every food I see."

NEW YORK JETS TACKLE **WINSTON HILL**, ON HIS EATING HABITS

"Pain is only temporary, no matter how long it lasts."

BALTIMORE RAVENS LINEBACKER RAY LEWIS

"No matter what your age, you're either going to be a head coach or you're not. If you wait five years, you still have to make that adjustment. If you're capable of doing it, you can do it now."

TV COMMENTATOR JOHN MADDEN, WHO WAS HIRED AS COACH
OF THE OAKLAND RAIDERS AT AGE 32 IN 1969

"I'm going to become a hog farmer. After some of the things I've been through, I regard it as a step up."

FORMER RICE UNIVERSITY COACH AL CONOVER

"Gentlemen, you are about to play Harvard for Yale. Never again in your lives will you do anything so important."

YALE UNIVERSITY FOOTBALL COACH TAD JONES

"If they retired the numbers of all the greats at Notre Dame, there wouldn't be any numbers left."

NOTRE DAME QUARTERBACK TERRY HANRATTY

"When you're playing for the national championship, it's not a matter of life or death. It's more important than that."

MICHIGAN STATE FOOTBALL COACH DUFFY DAUGHERTY

"This job is better than I could get if I used my college degree, which, at this point, I can't remember what it was in."

CLEVELAND BROWNS NOSE TACKLE BOB GOLIC,
AFTER SIGNING A TWO-YEAR, $1.5 MILLION CONTRACT

"The players on the Maryland football team all made straight As. Their Bs were a little crooked."

BALTIMORE DISC JOCKEY JOHNNY WALKER

"I never graduated from Iowa. I was only there for two terms — Truman's and Eisenhower's."

DETROIT LIONS DEFENSIVE LINEMAN ALEX KARRAS

"When I went duck hunting with Bear Bryant, he shot at one but it kept flying. 'John,' he said, 'there flies a dead duck.' Now that's confidence."

USC COACH JOHN MCKAY, ON HIS ALABAMA COUNTERPART

"Even if we had to pick up Joe en masse and carry him over the goal line, we were going to get a touchdown."

SAN FRANCISCO 49ERS GUARD RANDY CROSS, ON THE CONFIDENCE QUARTERBACK
JOE MONTANA INSPIRED WHILE DRIVING THE TEAM 92 YARDS FOR THE WINNING TOUCHDOWN
IN THE DYING MOMENTS OF SUPER BOWL XXIII

"It got to the point where, being a Christian and being a person who loves people, I actually felt sorry for the Broncos."

SAN FRANCISCO 49ERS TACKLE BUBBA PARIS ON SAN FRANCISCO'S
55-10 ROUT OF DENVER IN SUPER BOWL XXIV

"There's one voice for discipline. Mine. There's one voice for leadership. Mine."

DETROIT LIONS HEAD COACH ROD MARINELLI, A VIETNAM VETERAN,
AT THE PRESS CONFERENCE TO ANNOUNCE HIS HIRING

"My father really believed in discipline. So did my mother. Till I was thirteen, I thought my name was 'Shut up.'"

NEW YORK JETS QUARTERBACK JOE NAMATH

"Which eye?"

REPLY FROM WASHINGTON REDSKINS QUARTERBACK SAMMY BAUGH TO INSTRUCTIONS
FROM COACH RAY FLAHERTY TO HIT THE END IN THE EYE WITH THE BALL

"I'm the best defensive end around. I'd hate to have to play against me."

LOS ANGELES RAMS STAR DEACON JONES

"Yeah, they gave me the game ball. If they hadn't given it to me, I would have taken it anyway."

DETROIT LIONS LINEBACKER MIKE LUCCI, AFTER THREE KEY INTERCEPTIONS
AGAINST THE CHICAGO BEARS

"If I'm not selected for the Pro Bowl this year, Stevie Wonder must be counting the ballots."

CHICAGO BEARS LINEBACKER OTIS WILSON, ON HIS PLAY DURING THE 1985 SEASON

"I don't care how complicated they make the game seem, it's really based on two principles, and those are blocking and tackling."

CHICAGO BEARS HALL OF FAME HALFBACK RED GRANGE

"You don't have to win it, just don't lose it."

BALTIMORE RAVENS LINEBACKER RAY LEWIS, TO QUARTERBACK ELVIS GRBAC

"It's not whether you win or lose, it's who gets the blame."

DALLAS COWBOYS LINEMAN BLAINE NYE

"I'm not the one who got tired in the Super Bowl."

PHILADELPHIA EAGLES RECEIVER TERRELL OWENS,
TAKING ANOTHER SHOT AT DONOVAN MCNABB P52

"If God wanted women to understand men, football would never have been created."

WRITER ROGER SIMON

"It's sort of like a beauty contest. It's very easy to pick the top one, two or three girls, but then the rest of them look the same. It's like that in scouting."

PRO FOOTBALL SCOUT GIL BRANDT

"A **bowling ball** rolling **downhill**."

DENVER BRONCOS DEFENSIVE LINEMAN GERARD WARREN, DESCRIBING PITTSBURG STEELERS RUNNING BACK JEROME BETTIS

"He's like a beautiful woman who can't cook, doesn't want to clean and doesn't want to take care of the kids. You really don't want her, but she's so beautiful that you can't let her go."

PLAYER TURNED TV COMMENTATOR DEION SANDERS, COMMENTING ON PROBLEM RECEIVER RANDY MOSS

"Tom Landry is a perfectionist. If he was married to Raquel Welch, he'd expect her to cook."

DALLAS COWBOYS QUARTERBACK DON MEREDITH, ON HIS COACH

"Boats. Planes. Cars. Clothes. Blondes. Brunettes. Redheads. All so pretty. I love them all."

NEW YORK JETS PLAYBOY QUARTERBACK JOE NAMATH

"Who wants to go with a guy who's got two bad knees and a quick release?"

ACTRESS CONNIE STEVENS, ON JOE NAMATH

"I recruited a Czech kicker, and during the eye examination, the doctor asked him if he could read the bottom line. 'Read it!' the Czech kicker said, 'I know him.'"

OHIO STATE FOOTBALL COACH WOODY HAYES

"You battle for 59 minutes, and then some little guy with a clean uniform comes in to kick a field goal to win the game, and he says, 'Hooray, I keek a touchdown.'"

DETROIT LIONS DEFENSIVE TACKLE ALEX KARRAS, DERIDING KICKERS LIKE HIS TEAMMATE
GARO YEPREMIAN OF CYPRUS, WHO LATER USED THIS AS THE TITLE OF HIS AUTOBIOGRAPHY

"They ought to tighten the immigration laws."

MINNESOTA VIKINGS COACH NORM VAN BROCKLIN, AFTER DETROIT'S GARO YEPREMIAN
KICKED SIX FIELD GOALS TO BEAT HIS TEAM

"I don't hire anybody not brighter than I am. If they're not brighter than I am, I don't need them."

UNIVERSITY OF ALABAMA FOOTBALL COACH PAUL (BEAR) BRYANT

"A good coach needs a patient wife, a loyal dog, and a great quarterback, but not necessarily in that order."

MINNESOTA VIKINGS COACH BUD GRANT

"If they want to use artificial turf, let them find artificial players."

MIAMI DOLPHINS LINEBACKER DOUG SWIFT

"Mug him on the way out of the locker room."

NEW YORK GIANTS LINEBACKER SAM HUFF, ON HOW TO STOP LEGENDARY CLEVELAND BROWNS
RUNNING BACK JIM BROWN

"You could give your outside linebackers hand grenades."

CLEVELAND BROWNS COACH **SAM RUTIGLIANO**, WHEN ASKED HOW TO STOP SEATTLE
QUARTERBACK JIM ZORN FROM SCRAMBLING

"We're going to win Sunday. I'll guarantee you."

NEW YORK JETS QUARTERBACK **JOE NAMATH**, ON THE THURSDAY BEFORE SUPER 30WL III
AGAINST THE 21-POINT FAVORITE BALTIMORE COLTS

"I left because of illness and fatigue. The fans were sick and
tired of me."

FORMER DENVER BRONCOS COACH **JOHN RALSTON**

"You can have three great seasons and then lose, and it's
'What have you done for me lately?'"

BIG EAST COMMISSIONER **MIKE TRANGHESE**, EXPLAINING WHY HE THINKS
THERE'LL BE NO MORE COACHES WITH THE LONGEVITY OF PENN STATE'S JOE PATERNO

"Every coach is in the last year of his contract. Some just
don't know it."

CAROLINA PANTHERS OFFENSIVE COORDINATOR (AND FORMER FALCONS
AND CHARGERS HEAD COACH) **DAN HENNING**

"If you're a coach, NFL stands for 'Not For Long.'"

NFL COACH TURNED TV COMMENTATOR **JERRY GLANVILLE**

"This is the best place for guys to come and focus on nothing but football."

PACKERS QUARTERBACK **BRETT FAVRE** ON PLAYING IN GREEN BAY

"The street to obscurity is paved with athletes who perform great feats before friendly crowds. Greatness in major league sports is the ability to win in a stadium filled with people who are pulling for you to lose."

WASHINGTON REDSKINS COACH **GEORGE ALLEN**

"When you come to Pittsburgh you are playing forty players and 50,000 fans."

PITTSBURGH STEELERS RUNNING BACK **FRENCHY FUQUA**

"Sure, the home field is an advantage — but so is having a lot of talent."

MIAMI DOLPHINS QUARTERBACK **DAN MARINO**

"We're so far away from most of the country, only Lewis and Clark know where we are."

SEATTLE SEAHAWKS VICE PRESIDENT **GARY WRIGHT**, ON HIS TEAM'S LACK OF MEDIA ATTENTION

"There's no system of play that substitutes for knocking an opponent down. When you hit, hit hard."

FOOTBALL COACH **POP WARNER**

If my mother put on a helmet and shoulder pads and a uniform that wasn't the same one I was wearing, I'd run over her if she was in my way. And I love my mother.

LOS ANGELES RAIDERS RUNNING BACK (AND MULTI-SPORT STAR) BO JACKSON

"I had a license to kill for 60 minutes a week. It was like going totally insane."

DETROIT LIONS DEFENSIVE LINEMAN **ALEX KARRAS**

"I like to believe that my best hits border on felonious assault."

OAKLAND RAIDERS DEFENSIVE BACK **JACK TATUM**, WHO WAS KNOWN AS "THE ASSASSIN"

"We try to hurt everybody. We hit each other as hard as we can. This is a man's game."

NEW YORK GIANTS LINEBACKER **SAM HUFF**

"He knocks the hell out of people, but in a Christian way."

WASHINGTON REDSKINS QUARTERBACK (AND TEXAS CHRISTIAN UNIVERSITY ALUM)
SAMMY BAUGH, ON A VERY RELIGIOUS LINEBACKER

"I guess people think the Bears keep me in a cage and only let me out on Sundays to play football. Nobody thinks I can talk, much less write my own name."

LEGENDARY CHICAGO BEARS LINEBACKER **DICK BUTKUS**,
WHO DID NOT APPRECIATE HIS NICKNAME "THE ANIMAL"

"Football is not a contact sport. Football is a collision sport. Dancing is a contact sport."

MICHIGAN STATE FOOTBALL COACH DUFFY DAUGHERTY

"It's gotten to the point where I can't say something in jest without being taken seriously."

DALLAS COWBOYS QUARTERBACK ROGER STAUBACH, ON HIS CLEAN-CUT IMAGE

"The only perfect man who ever lived had a beard and long hair and didn't wear shoes and slept in barns and didn't hold a regular job and never put on a tie. I'm not comparing myself to Him – I'm in enough trouble trying to stack up against Bart Starr – but I'm saying that you don't judge a man by the way he cuts his hair. Shoot, I never saw a picture of a saint who didn't have long hair. Abraham Lincoln had a beard, and George Washington wore a wig."

NEW YORK JETS QUARTERBACK JOE NAMATH, DEFENDING HIS HAIRSTYLE
AGAINST THE CONSERVATIVE NFL ESTABLISHMENT

"I don't know what he has. A pulled groin. A hip flexor. I don't know. A pulled something. I never pulled anything. You can't pull fat."

NEW YORK JETS COACH BRUCE COSLET

"When you get old, everything is hurting. When I get up in the morning, it sounds like I'm making popcorn."

NEW YORK GIANTS LINEBACKER **LAWRENCE TAYLOR**

"John Riggins, like Joe Namath, is a riddle wrapped in a bandage."

SPORTS COMMENTATOR **LARRY MERCHANT**

"When Nature designed the male knee, she obviously had neither football nor walking shorts in mind."

WRITER **BILL VAUGHAN**

"Joe has a 22-year-old body and 70-year-old knees."

A NEW YORK JETS TEAMMATE, ON **JOE NAMATH**

"Physically, he's a world-beater. Mentally, he's an egg-beater."

UNIVERSITY OF MICHIGAN CENTER **MATT ELLIOTT**,
DESCRIBING OHIO STATE LINEBACKER ALONZO SPELLMAN

"The scouts said I looked like Tarzan and played like Jane."

PHILADELPHIA EAGLES 6'8", 275-POUND DEFENSIVE END **DENNIS HARRISON**,
ON WHY HE WAS PASSED OVER IN THE FIRST THREE ROUNDS OF THE 1978 NFL DRAFT

"I have a pair of legs that only an orthopedic surgeon could love."

NEW YORK JETS QUARTERBACK JOE NAMATH

"I'm cool on the outside, but on the inside it's like a thousand little kids jumping up and down on Christmas morning."

MINNESOTA VIKING **CHUCK FOREMAN**, WHO DID NOT CELEBRATE HIS TOUCHDOWNS

"My knees look like they lost a knife fight with a midget."

KANSAS CITY CHIEFS LINEBACKER **E.J. HOLUB**, AFTER HIS TWELFTH KNEE OPERATION

"The pads don't keep you from getting hurt. They just keep you from getting killed."

INDIANAPOLIS COLTS DEFENSIVE END **CHAD BRATZKE**

"Ever since they put this pin in I've been getting great reception on my car radio. I wonder what will happen when I try to get on an airplane?"

MIAMI DOLPHIN **BOB KUECHENBERG**, ON PLAYING WITH A STEEL PIN IN HIS BROKEN ARM

"When you're around Ben, he's much more mature than his age would indicate."

PITTSBURG STEELERS COACH BILL COWHER, ON QB BEN ROETHLISBERGER'S PERFORMANCE IN THE 2006 AFC CHAMPIONSHIP

"If they don't want 'em to get hit, why don't they just put a dress on 'em?"

PITTSBURGH STEELERS LINEBACKER **JACK LAMBERT**, ON QUARTERBACKS

"It's like being in a huddle with God."

BALTIMORE COLTS TIGHT END **JOHN MACKEY**, ON HALL OF FAME QUARTERBACK JOHNNY UNITAS

"It's like holding group therapy for 50,000 people a week."

WASHINGTON REDSKIN **SONNY JURGENSEN**, ON PLAYING QUARTERBACK

"He is to passing what Lindbergh was to the airplane."

FOOTBALL HISTORIAN **KEVIN ROBERTS**, ON WASHINGTON REDSKINS
QUARTERBACK SAMMY BAUGH

"Dick Butkus was like Moby Dick in a goldfish bowl."

NFL FILMS PRESIDENT **STEVE SABOL**

"He's like a state fair. He gets bigger and better every year."

NEW ORLEANS SAINTS QUARTERBACK **ARCHIE MANNING** (FATHER OF PEYTON AND ELI),
ON LOS ANGELES RAMS VETERAN DEFENSIVE TACKLE MERLIN OLSEN

"It was as if a locomotive had hit me and been followed by a ten-ton truck rambling over the remains."

NOTRE DAME FOOTBALL COACH **KNUTE ROCKNE**, RECALLING WHAT IT HAD BEEN LIKE TO PLAY
AGAINST JIM THORPE

"It was like having a redwood tree fall on you."

CHICAGO BEARS OWNER, COACH AND FORMER PLAYER GEORGE HALAS,
ON HIS MEMORIES OF BEING TACKLED BY JIM THORPE

"Tackling Bronko was like trying to stop a freight train going downhill."

FOOTBALL LEGEND ERNIE NEVERS, ON BRONKO NAGURSKI

"One thing I've learned over the years is sometimes if you make kicks early in the game, you don't have to make them late."

KICKER GARY ANDERSON, THE NFL'S ALL-TIME SCORING LEADER

"I'd rather win 55–0 if you want to know the truth."

SEATTLE SEAHAWKS KICKER JOSH BROWN, ON HIS FEELINGS ABOUT A CHANCE
TO KICK THE GAME-WINNING FIELD GOAL IN SUPER BOWL XL

"He plays middle linebacker like a piranha."

SCOUT AND FUTURE NEW YORK JETS COACH JOE WALTON,
ON DICK BUTKUS OF THE CHICAGO BEARS

"Other guys like Baltimore's Mike Curtis and Chicago's Dick Butkus thrive on that man-eating image. I never have cared for it."

MIAMI DOLPHINS LINEBACKER NICK BUONICONTI, WHO ENJOYED A HALL OF FAME CAREER
WHILE WORKING AS A LAWYER IN THE OFF-SEASON

"I've been a quarterback since high school. I've always been black."

WASHINGTON REDSKIN **DOUG WILLIAMS**, ANSWERING THE QUESTION "HOW LONG HAVE YOU BEEN A BLACK QUARTERBACK?"

"If they did, I'd stomp 'em and do a pirouette on their heads."

CINCINNATI BENGALS LINEBACKER **KEN AVERY**, WHEN ASKED IF ANYONE EVER CALLED HIM A SISSY BECAUSE HE STUDIED BALLET

"Playing middle linebacker is like walking through a lion's cage in a three-piece porkchop suit."

TAMPA BAY BUCCANEERS LINEBACKER **CECIL JOHNSON**

"Gentlemen, this is a football."

GREEN BAY PACKERS COACH **VINCE LOMBARDI**, HOLDING UP A BALL IN FRONT OF HIS PLAYERS AND LETTING THEM KNOW IT WAS TIME TO GET BACK TO BASICS

"There is Eastern Standard Time and Greenwich Time and then there is Lombardi Time – fifteen minutes early. If you come ten minutes early, they've started without you."

GREEN BAY PACKERS KICKER **DON CHANDLER**

"There's a second-place bowl game, and it's a hinky-dink football game, held in a hinky-dink town, played by hinky-dink football players. That's all second place is: hinky-dink."

VINCE LOMBARDI

"The spirit, the will to win, and the will to excel are the things that endure. These qualities are so much more important than the events that occur."

VINCE LOMBARDI

"Lombardi treats us all the same — like dogs."

GREEN BAY PACKERS DEFENSIVE TACKLE **HENRY JORDAN**

"When he says sit down, I don't even bother to look for a chair."

GREEN BAY PACKERS TIGHT END **MAX MCGEE**, ON VINCE LOMBARDI

"He united us, initially, in our fear of him, our hatred for him. He was, deliberately, the common enemy, the focus of all our frustrations. If our muscles ached, it was Lombardi's fault. If our nerves were frayed, it was Lombardi's fault. If our mind reeled, it was Lombardi's fault. The fierceness of Lombardi, combined with the smallness of the city in which we played, forced upon us camaraderie and a closeness that, nurtured by victory, grew into love."

GREEN BAY PACKERS GUARD AND AUTHOR **JERRY KRAMER**

"One night, after a long, cold difficult day, Lombardi came home late and tumbled into bed. 'God,' said his wife, 'your feet are cold.' And Lombardi answered, 'Around the house, dear, you may call me Vince.'"

GREEN BAY PACKERS HALFBACK **PAUL HORNUNG**, ON VINCE LOMBARDI

"Sure, luck means a lot in football. Not having a good quarterback is bad luck."

MIAMI DOLPHINS COACH **DON SHULA**

"By nature, I'm aggressive. I'll take shots, I'll take chances; therefore, you have mistakes."

GREEN BAY PACKERS QUARTERBACK **BRETT FAVRE**,
ON WHY HE THROWS SO MANY INTERCEPTIONS

"OK, it's a risk. But hey, I'm a poker player. You can take it to the river. I'm not scared to make a change. I'm not scared to go out on a limb and try something different."

FORMER INDIANAPOLIS COLTS RUNNING BACK **EDGERRIN JAMES**,
ON HIS DECISION TO SIGN WITH THE ARIZONA CARDINALS

"Maybe the difference in football is your mistakes come in front of several million people. Most people's mistakes are buried someplace."

WASHINGTON REDSKINS COACH **JOE GIBBS**

"You have a chance to make a big play, you take it. Because you don't know when you'll get your next opportunity. It's not like I'm thinking, waiting, 'Well, should I do it, shouldn't I do it?' You just react."

FORMER MIAMI DOLPHINS QUARTERBACK **DAN MARINO**,
ATTRIBUTING HIS SUCCESS TO AN ABSENCE OF FEAR

"Some coaches pray for wisdom. I pray for 260-pound tackles. They'll give me plenty of wisdom."

WAKE FOREST UNIVERSITY COACH **CHUCK MILLS**

"No player is wortha million dollars. I can understand why a player would have an agent. I couldn't keep from laughing if I went in and demanded a million from an owner."

CHICAGO BEARS LEGEND RED GRANGE

"I gave George Allen an unlimited budget and he exceeded it."

WASHINGTON REDSKINS OWNER EDWARD BENNETT WILLIAMS,
ON WHY HE FIRED HIS HEAD COACH

"A lot of players didn't have agents then. We couldn't understand why we should pay an agent a commission for not getting us the same salary we couldn't get on our own."

PITTSBURGH STEELERS QUARTERBACK TURNED COMMENTATOR TERRY BRADSHAW,
ON CONTRACT NEGOTIATIONS IN THE EARLY 1970S

"Agents today make more money for negotiating rookie contracts than I made for playing."

PITTSBURGH STEELERS QUARTERBACK TURNED COMMENTATOR TERRY BRADSHAW

"The irony is that the sport with the most devastating rate of injury has the least guarantees."

AGENT LEIGH STEINBERG, ON THE LACK OF GUARANTEED CONTRACTS IN THE NFL

"I'm the one you need to be worried about."

TATTOO ON THE LEFT BICEPS OF PITSBURG STEELERS LINEBACKER LARRY FOOTE

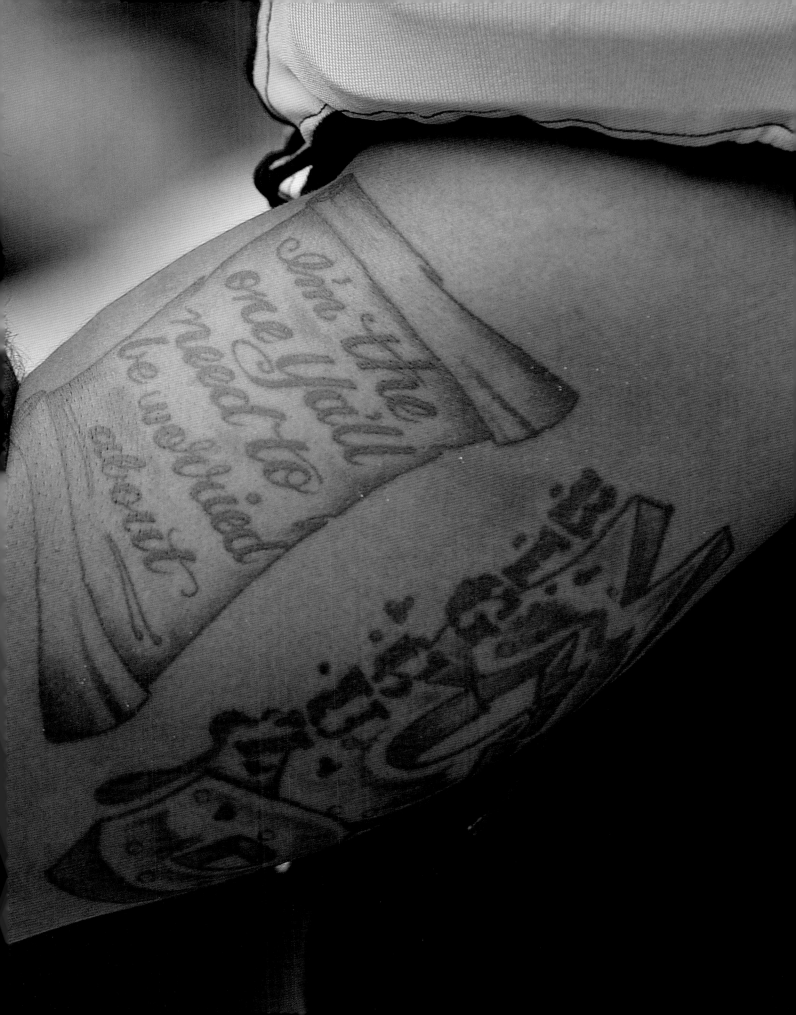

"If he doesn't sign, we lose him. If he does sign, I go broke."

ATLANTA FALCONS OWNER **RANKIN SMITH**, ON THE TROUBLE SIGNING DRAFT CHOICES DURING THE DAYS OF THE WORLD FOOTBALL LEAGUE

"I got a million-dollar offer from the WFL — one dollar a year for a million years."

JOURNEYMAN OFFENSIVE TACKLE **STEVE WRIGHT**, ON A BIG-MONEY OFFER FROM THE RIVAL WORLD FOOTBALL LEAGUE

"I never thought my biggest worry would be income taxes."

DALLAS COWBOYS DEFENSIVE TACKLE **BOB LILLY**

"Players are different today. They don't understand that it's a privilege to play this game. It's an honor. You have an opportunity to make a lot of money. But when you're complaining about only making $7 million to feed your family, nobody has sympathy for that. You're going to turn people off."

FORMER DALLAS COWBOYS RUNNING BACK **TONY DORSETT**

"It's basically receiver money. David wants to be a receiver in this league and feels he should be paid receiver money."

AGENT **MARK CLOUSER**, ON THE NEW FIVE-YEAR CONTRACT FOR NEW YORK GIANT DAVID TYREE THAT MADE HIM THE NFL'S HIGHEST-PAID SPECIAL TEAMS PLAYER

"What I find sometimes is that all of us may have too much money. Players. Owners. TV. It's like pigs fighting in a trough, and sometimes we don't appreciate what we have."

NFL EXECUTIVE **MIKE BROWN**

"Anybody who says they aren't in it for the money is full of sh*t."

OAKLAND RAIDERS RECEIVER **FRED BILETNIKOFF**

"Nobody in football should be called a genius. A genius is a guy like Norman Einstein."

WASHINGTON REDSKINS QUARTERBACK TURNED COMMENTATOR **JOE THEISMANN**,
WHO HAD A CHILDHOOD FRIEND NAMED NORMAN EINSTEIN

"We had no painkillers in those days. Nothing. You lived with pain. I don't think there was ever a ballgame that most of us didn't live with pain. But you were so wrought-up playing the game that you didn't think about it. Outside of getting a little rest now and then, the one and only time I ever left a game was when Bronko Nagurski put seven stitches in my face. They took me down to the emergency room of the hospital and put the stitches in, and they brought me back in a taxicab and I went back into the ballgame."

GREEN BAY PACKERS FULLBACK **CLARKE HINKLE**

"**IF ME AND KING KONG WENT INTO AN ALLEY, ONLY ONE OF US WOULD COME OUT. AND IT WOULDN'T BE THE MONKEY.**"

DEFENSIVE LINEMAN LYLE ALZADO, KNOWN FOR HIS FIERCE PLAY WITH THE DENVER BRONCOS, CLEVELAND BROWNS AND LOS ANGELES RAIDERS

"Mark Gastineau has got an IQ of about room temperature."

CHICAGO BEARS DEFENSIVE LINEMAN **DAN HAMPTON**, ON HIS NEW YORK JETS RIVAL

"Every time you make a football player think, you're handicappin' him."

HOUSTON OILERS COACH **BUM PHILLIPS**

"In other jobs, you get old, big deal. In football, you get old, you're fired. That's what happened to me. Time got me. Damned time."

LOS ANGELES RAMS HALL OF FAME DEFENSIVE END **DEACON JONES**

"For a while you're a veteran, and then you're just old."

SAN DIEGO CHARGERS RECEIVER **LANCE ALWORTH**

"The older you get, the faster you ran when you were a kid."

NEW YORK GIANTS COACH **STEVE OWEN**

"I've got one advantage — when you're as slow as I am, you don't lose any steps as you grow older."

MIAMI DOLPHINS VETERAN RECEIVER **HOWARD TWILLEY**

"We professional athletes are very lucky. Unlike most mortals, we are given the privilege of dying twice — once when we retire and again when death takes us."

GREEN BAY PACKERS HALFBACK **JOHNNY (BLOOD) MCNALLY**

"I knew it was time to quit when I was chewing out an official and he walked off the penalty faster than I could keep up with him."

CHICAGO BEARS OWNER AND COACH GEORGE HALAS, ON WHY HE GAVE UP COACHING

"I was able to push the pain down, lock it in until the game was over. I didn't know it then, but pain would be with me the rest of my life. Toward the end of my career, my joints hurt so much on Monday morning after a game that I would sometimes have to crawl from bed to the bathroom."

CHICAGO BEARS LINEBACKER DICK BUTKUS

"In this game all you need is speed, strength and an ability to recognize pain immediately."

CINCINNATI BENGALS LINEBACKER REGGIE WILLIAMS

"You don't take yourself too seriously when you're winning, and you don't beat yourself up when you lose some games."

PITTSBURGH STEELERS COACH BILL COWHER

"Pro football gave me a good perspective. When I entered the political arena, I had already been booed, cheered, cut, sold, traded, and hung in effigy."

BUFFALO BILLS QUARTERBACK TURNED U.S. CONGRESSMAN JACK KEMP

"The world doesn't stop turning. Eventually your time runs out."

MIAMI DOLPHIN **GUS FREROTTE**, ON HELPING TO PREPARE A YOUNG QUARTERBACK
TO TAKE HIS JOB ONE DAY

"If Marc Bulger throws an interception in Sun Devil Stadium
and nobody is there to see it, is it still an interception?"

ST. LOUIS POST-DISPATCH WRITER **JEFF GORDON**, ON THE POOR ATTENDANCE
AT ARIZONA CARDINALS GAMES

"If 'ifs' and 'buts' were candy and nuts,
wouldn't it be a Merry Christmas."

DALLAS COWBOYS QUARTERBACK TURNED TV COMMENTATOR **DON MEREDITH**

"It's like when you have three wheels for a bike and you only
need two. One has to lean against the wall. Well, here I am."

WASHINGTON REDSKINS QUARTERBACK **JOE THEISMANN**, ON GOING FROM A STARTER
WITH THE CFL'S TORONTO ARGONAUTS TO THIRD STRING IN THE NFL

"Old place-kickers never die, they just go on missing the
point."

HALL OF FAME KICKER **LOU (THE TOE) GROZA**

"It is better to be devoured by lions than to be eaten by dogs."

NORTHWESTERN UNIVERSITY FOOTBALL COACH **ALEX AGASE**,
EXPLAINING WHY HIS TEAMS PLAYED DIFFICULT SCHEDULES

"When it rains it pours. All you can do is put your buckets out in the house when it's leaking and try to do the best you can."

CAROLINA PANTHERS RECEIVER STEVE SMITH, ON HIS TEAM'S TOUGH TIME
AGAINST SEATTLE IN THE 2006 NFC CHAMPIONSHIP

"What's one more torpedo in a sinking ship?"

GREEN BAY PACKERS QUARTERBACK LYNN DICKEY, WHEN ASKED WHY HE WAS STILL PLAYING
FOOTBALL AFTER HAVING SUFFERED A DISLOCATED HIPBONE, SHATTERED HIP SOCKET,
BROKEN FIBULA, AND A VARIETY OF OTHER INJURIES

"Football kickers are like taxicabs. You can always go out and hire another one."

CHICAGO BEARS DEFENSIVE COACH BUDDY RYAN

"Always have a plan and believe in it. I tell my coaches not to compromise. Nothing good happens by accident."

SEATTLE SEAHAWKS COACH CHUCK KNOX

"You can't go out and practice average on Wednesday, average on Thursday, okay on Friday and then expect to play well on Sunday."

NEW ENGLAND PATRIOTS QUARTERBACK TOM BRADY

"In practice, I run every play like I'm scoring a touchdown."

MIAMI DOLPHINS RUNNING BACK MERCURY MORRIS

"Most football players are temperamental. That's 90 percent temper and 10 percent mental."
FORMER CHICAGO BEARS SAFETY **DOUG PLANK**

"Playing in the NFL is 10 percent mental, 90 percent Hollywood."
PHILADELPHIA EAGLES RECEIVER **TERRELL OWENS**

"If I was a goody-goody, I'd be a psychological wreck."
LEGENDARY CLEVELAND BROWNS RUNNING BACK **JIM BROWN**,
ON HIS LIFE OFF THE FOOTBALL FIELD

"Everybody is not going to be squeaky clean."
TROUBLEMAKING RECEIVER **TERRELL OWENS**

"I don't think I've been asked this many questions since my mother caught me drinking in high school."
MIAMI DOLPHINS THIRD-STRING QUARTERBACK **DON STROCK**,
FACING THE MEDIA AFTER HIS FIRST START

"You have to play this game like somebody just hit your mother with a two-by-four."
OAKLAND RAIDERS DEFENSIVE LINEMAN **DAN BIRDWELL**

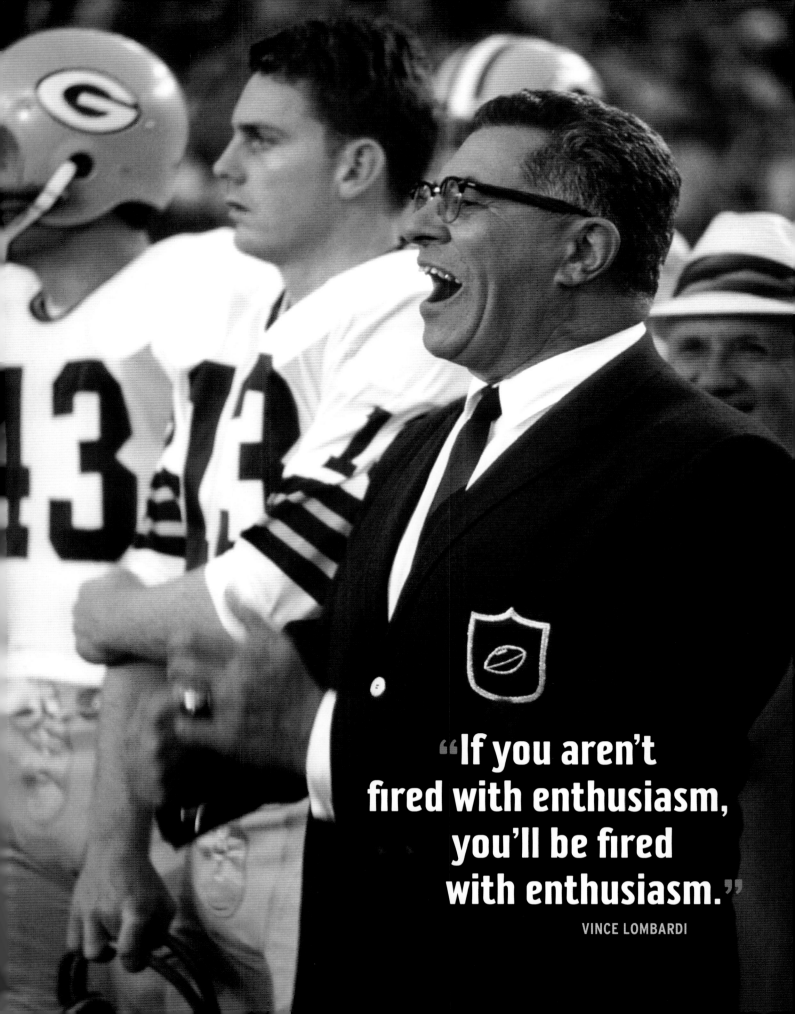

"If you aren't fired with enthusiasm, you'll be fired with enthusiasm."

VINCE LOMBARDI

"The minute you think you've got it made, disaster is just around the corner."

PENN STATE COACH JOE PATERNO

"Frank Leahy was here for three years and went to war. I think sometimes that would be a welcome relief to get away from the pressures."

LOU HOLTZ, ON THE PRESSURE OF COACHING AT NOTRE DAME

"Most train to be part of the game. The greatest train to be the game: I am the game. Third-and-9, two minutes left, that's what I train for. I train for moments everyone runs from. I run to them."

DALLAS COWBOYS RECEIVER MICHAEL IRVIN

"I like to just sit and watch him."

CHICAGO BEARS QUARTERBACK SID LUCKMAN, ON HIS WASHINGTON REDSKINS RIVAL SAMMY BAUGH

"I'd run over my own mother to win the Super Bowl."

WASHINGTON REDSKINS LINEMAN JOE JACOBY, BEFORE SUPER BOWL XVIII VERSUS THE RAIDERS

"To win, I'd run over Joe's mom, too."

LOS ANGELES RAIDERS LINEBACKER MATT MILLEN

"Johnny Unitas is the greatest quarterback ever to play the game, better than I was, better than Sammy Baugh, better than anyone."

CHICAGO BEARS QUARTERBACK SID LUCKMAN

"The only qualifications for a lineman are to be big and dumb. To be a back you only have to be dumb."

NOTRE DAME FOOTBALL COACH KNUTE ROCKNE

"Let's face it. The reason you're playing offense is because you ain't good enough to play defense. When you play guard, it's because you aren't smart enough to be a quarterback, not fast enough to be a halfback, not rugged enough to be a fullback, not big enough to be a tackle, and you don't have the hands of an end."

UNIVERSITY OF GEORGIA OFFENSIVE LINE COACH DICK BESTWICK

"He's big as a gorilla and strong as a gorilla. Now, if he was smart as a gorilla, he'd be fine."

UNIVERSITY OF ALABAMA ASSISTANT COACH SAM BAILEY, ON A FRESHMAN PLAYER

"In Montana, they renamed a town after an all-time great, Joe Montana. Well, a town in Massachusetts changed their name to honor my guy Terry Bradshaw — Marblehead."

PLAYER TURNED TV COMMENTATOR HOWIE LONG, JOKING WITH FOX COLLEAGUE AND FORMER PITTSBURGH STEELERS QUARTERBACK TERRY BRADSHAW

"He couldn't spell 'cat' if you spotted him the C and the A."

DALLAS COWBOYS LINEBACKER THOMAS (HOLLYWOOD) HENDERSON, TAKING A SHOT AT THE INTELLIGENCE OF PITTSBURG STEELERS QB TERRY BRADSHAW PRIOR TO SUPER BOWL XIII

"I may be dumb, but I'm not stupid."

TERRY BRADSHAW

"Pressure is something you feel when you don't know what the hell you're doing."

INDIANAPOLIS COLTS QUARTERBACK **PEYTON MANNING**

"In his worst games, Baugh is as good as most quarterbacks on their best days."

FOOTBALL HISTORIAN **ROGER TREAT**, ON WASHINGTON REDSKINS QUARTERBACK SAMMY BAUGH

"Sometimes a guy's just a normal guy, but he's got a Microsoft brain."

SAN FRANCISCO 49ERS CORNERBACK **RONNIE LOTT**, ON QUARTERBACK JOE MONTANA

"You could beat Bradshaw half to death, but there'd still be enough life in him to kill you."

WASHINGTON REDSKINS COACH **GEORGE ALLEN**, ON PITTSBURGH STEELERS QUARTERBACK TERRY BRADSHAW

"Bart's big thing was knowing what he had to do and how to do it. When he called the play, there were no doubters in the huddle."

GREEN BAY PACKERS OFFENSIVE TACKLE **FORREST GREGG**, ON QUARTERBACK BART STARR

"A quarterback hasn't arrived until he can tell the coach to go to hell."

BALTIMORE COLTS QUARTERBACK JOHNNY UNITAS

"No one ever saw John Unitas sliding into the grass after a scramble to avoid being tackled. Quarterbacks who did that were automatically labeled a sissy."

BALTIMORE COLTS DEFENSIVE LINEMAN ART DONOVAN

"He can't run, he can't pass, and he can't kick — all he can do is beat you."

UNIVERSITY OF ALABAMA FOOTBALL COACH PAUL (BEAR) BRYANT,
ON CRIMSON TIDE QUARTERBACK PAT TRAMMEL

"I didn't get the ring, but I did get the Super Bowl pay bonus. I was happy about that. I'll take the bonus over the ring any day."

NEW ENGLAND PATRIOTS RESERVE TIGHT END ZERON FLEMISTER,
WHO MISSED THE ENTIRE 2004 SEASON WITH A TORN ACHILLES TENDON

"You can go to the bank and borrow money, but you can't go to the bank and borrow a Super Bowl ring."

PITTSBURGH STEELERS DEFENSIVE LINEMAN MEAN JOE GREENE

"He was most dangerous when you thought you had him. He'd gather himself up and you'd find yourself empty-handed."

"He looks no different than any other runner when he's coming at you, but when he gets there, he's gone."

"Franco Harris faked me out so bad one time that I got a 15-yard penalty for grabbing my own face mask."

"You need two yards, I'll get you three. You need 10 yards, I'll get you three."

"There were a lot of running backs as good as me. The real difference was that I could focus. I never laid back and relied on natural ability."

"**There is a difference between conceit and confidence. A quarterback has to have confidence. Conceit is bragging about yourself. Confidence means you believe you can get the job done.**"

BALTIMORE COLTS QUARTERBACK JOHNNY UNITAS

"Football goes in cycles. Wide ties keep coming back again. So will the running game."

NEW ORLEANS SAINTS QUARTERBACK ARCHIE MANNING (FATHER OF PEYTON AND ELI), ON THE NFL IN THE EARLY 1980S

"We've got to keep it in retrospective."

BUFFALO BILLS QUARTERBACK JIM KELLY, WHOSE TEAM LOST THE SUPER BOWL FOUR YEARS IN A ROW

"You don't get hurt running straight ahead ... three-yards-and-a-cloud-of-dust offense. I will pound you and pound you until you quit."

OHIO STATE FOOTBALL COACH WOODY HAYES

"The forward pass has brought in so many complicated rules in the U.S. that much of their best ball-carrying is now done by the referees."

PLAYER, COACH AND SPORTSWRITER TED REEVES, ON THE INTRODUCTION OF FORWARD PASSING TO FOOTBALL IN EASTERN CANADA IN 1931

"Only three things can happen when you put a ball up in the air — and two of them are bad."

MICHIGAN STATE FOOTBALL COACH DUFFY DAUGHERTY

"When in doubt, punt."

LEGENDARY COLLEGE FOOTBALL COACH JOHN HEISMAN

"I don't know how drastic it is. That's up to people who measure drastic-ticity, or whatever the word is. Drastic-ticians."

TAMPA BAY BUCCANEERS COACH JON GRUDEN, ON THE TEAM GOING FROM WORST TO FIRST IN THE NFC SOUTH DIVISION IN 2005

"The only way to describe him was 'indescribable.'"

UNIVERSITY OF TENNESSEE HEAD COACH BILL BATTLE, ON QUARTERBACK CONDREDGE HOLLOWAY

"I've always said the sun doesn't shine on the same dog every day, but we sure as heck didn't expect a near total eclipse."

TEXAS TECH COACH STEVE SLOAN, AFTER HIS UNDEFEATED TEAM BARELY BEAT WINLESS TEXAS CHRISTIAN

"I knew I'd bounce back. I wasn't dead or anything."

SEATTLE SEAHAWKS RECEIVER DARRELL JACKSON, ON THE CONCUSSION HE SUFFERED DURING THE 2002 SEASON

"From the waist down, Earl Campbell has the biggest legs I have ever seen on a running back."

TV COMMENTATOR JOHN MADDEN

"If I drop dead tomorrow, at least I'll know I died in good health."

HOUSTON OILERS COACH BUM PHILLIPS, AFTER PASSING A PHYSICAL

"Statistics are a salve. You rub them on your wounds after you lose and you feel a little better."

CINCINNATI BENGALS COACH BILL (TIGER) JOHNSON

"We took the scenic route."

PITTSBURGH STEELERS LINEBACKER **JOEY PORTER**, ON THE TEAM'S DIFFICULT ROAD TO THE CHAMPIONSHIP AT SUPER BOWL XL

"There are no office hours for champions."

LOUISIANA STATE FOOTBALL COACH **PAUL DIETZEL**

"Winning isn't everything, but it beats anything that comes in second."

UNIVERSITY OF ALABAMA FOOTBALL COACH **PAUL (BEAR) BRYANT**

"Winning isn't everything; it's the only thing."

LEGENDARY GREEN BAY PACKERS COACH **VINCE LOMBARDI**

"He had a small window, but he hit the middle of the bull's-eye."

PITTSBURGH STEELERS RECEIVER HINES WARD, ON A TOUCHDOWN PASS THROWN
BY QUARTERBACK BEN ROETHLISBERGER

"I was always coming back unless I said I wasn't."

INDIANAPOLIS COLTS COACH TONY DUNGY, ANNOUNCING HE PLANNED TO RETURN AFTER
CONTEMPLATING RETIREMENT FOLLOWING THE 2005 SEASON

"When you're not done, you're not done. It's a hard feeling to describe."

FORMER UNIVERSITY OF NEBRASKA QUARTERBACK ERIC CROUCH, WHO WON THE HEISMAN
TROPHY IN 2001, HOPING TO RESTART HIS CAREER WITH THE TORONTO ARGONAUTS IN 2006

"I want to rush for 1,000 or 1,500 yards, whichever comes first."

NEW ORLEANS SAINTS RUNNING BACK GEORGE ROGERS,
ON HIS GOALS FOR THE UPCOMING SEASON

"He's the kind of player who usually comes along rarely and sometimes never."

MINNESOTA VIKINGS COACH BUD GRANT, ON DEFENSIVE TACKLE ALAN PAGE

"It's a once-in-a-lifetime thing that only happens every so often."

MINNESOTA VIKINGS RECEIVER RANDY MOSS, ON HIS NO-LOOK, OVER-THE-SHOULDER
LATERAL TO MOE WILLIAMS FOR A 59-YARD TOUCHDOWN

"I've been big ever since I was little."

"Probably the Beatles' White Album."

"He treats us like men.
He lets us wear earrings."

UNIVERSITY OF HOUSTON RECEIVER **TORRIN POLK**, ON COACH JOHN JENKINS

"I can't even count to 10 in English."

PITTSBURGH STEELERS RECEIVER **LEE MAYS**, WHEN ASKED BEFORE SUPER BOWL XL
IF HE COULD COUNT TO 10 IN A FOREIGN LANGUAGE

"It's kind of like comparing the Atlantic and Pacific oceans.
They'll both drown you."

KANSAS STATE COACH **JIM DICKEY**, WHEN ASKED TO COMPARE THE OKLAHOMA SOONERS
OF 1978 WITH THE 1977 TEAM

"Kansas State hasn't won a Big Eight championship in 40
years. I told them that if I don't win one in that same length
of time, I'll resign."

KANSAS STATE COACH **JIM DICKEY**

"It was a brain transplant. I got a sportswriter's brain so I could be sure I had one that hadn't been used."

MINNESOTA VIKINGS COACH NORM VAN BROCKLIN, WHEN ASKED ABOUT A RECENT OPERATION

"What's the difference between a three-week-old puppy and a sportswriter? In six weeks, the puppy stops whining."

CHICAGO BEARS COACH MIKE DITKA

"They say two things happen when you get older. One is you begin to forget things, and I can't remember what the other thing is."

80-YEAR-OLD BUFFALO BILLS GENERAL MANAGER MARV LEVY

"When the going gets tough, the tough get going."

UNIVERSITY OF ALABAMA FOOTBALL COACH PAUL (BEAR) BRYANT. (THIS QUOTE IS ATTRIBUTED TO MANY BUT WAS PROBABLY ORIGINATED BY BRYANT.)

"Training camp is tough, and there's some pain. But it's a good life. It's better than working."

CHICAGO BEARS DEFENSIVE END DOUG ATKINS

"In the 1950s, the players were tougher because they came out of World War II. We had a different mentality. We were raised to love your God, respect your elders, and fear no son-of-a-bitch that walks. It was survival of the fittest."

PHILADELPHIA EAGLES DEFENSIVE LINEMAN BUCKO KILROY

"I'm not trying to win a popularity poll. I'm trying to win football games. I don't like nice people. I like tough, honest people."

OHIO STATE FOOTBALL COACH WOODY HAYES

"Never overload your butt with your mouth."

SEATTLE SEAHAWKS COACH CHUCK KNOX

"If we'd listened to the experts, we shouldn't even bothered showing up."

NEW ENGLAND PATRIOTS DEFENSIVE LINEMAN WILLIE MCGINEST, ON THE TEAM'S UPSET OF THE ST. LOUIS RAMS IN SUPER BOWL XXXVI

"There is simply no way we can beat Notre Dame. But Notre Dame could lose to us."

GEORGIA TECH COACH PEPPER RODGERS

"It will take an act of God to beat us."

TORONTO ARGONAUTS COACH LEO CAHILL BEFORE A PLAYOFF GAME WITH THE OTTAWA ROUGH RIDERS. AFTER OVERNIGHT RAIN AND A HARD FROST, THE ARGOS LOST 32-3.

"A lot of people told him the world was flat, but he kept going until he found land."

PITTSBURGH STEELERS COACH BILL COWHER, COMPARING HIS TEAM'S DIFFICULT ROAD TO VICTORY IN SUPER BOWL XL TO CHRISTOPHER COLUMBUS' VOYAGE TO THE NEW WORLD

"I wouldn't ever set out to hurt anyone deliberately unless it was, you know, important — like a league game or something."

CHICAGO BEARS LINEBACKER DICK BUTKUS

"How would **you** like it if, at your job, **every time** you made the slightest **mistake** a little **red light** went **on** over your head and **18,000 people** stood up and **screamed at you?**"

HALL OF FAME CANADIENS GOALIE JACQUES PLANTE

"Every boo on the road is a cheer."

RED WINGS COACH SCOTTY BOWMAN

"It's not about what you did yesterday — it's what you do tomorrow. If you rely too much on yesterday, tomorrow is going to jump up and bite you in the pants."

FLYERS GOALIE JOHN VANBIESBROUCK, AFTER BEING BENCHED THE PREVIOUS NIGHT

"In the playoffs, will beats skill."

SHARKS COACH KEVIN CONSTANTINE

"We're going to be the best in the league at something. We're deep in anthem singers."

PREDATORS COACH BARRY TROTZ

"It's a terrible time of year to have a baby. Of course, she got married on draft day, so I think she has no idea what I do for a living."

NHL DIRECTOR OF OFFICIATING BRYAN LEWIS, ON HIS DAUGHTER EXPECTING
DURING THE PLAYOFFS

"Tasted like horse pee from a tin cup."

HALL OF FAME CANADIEN GOALIE GUMP WORSLEY, ON DRINKING CHAMPAGNE
FROM THE STANLEY CUP

136

"Some of us were meant to score, others were meant to play goal. And others were meant to do what I do. I tick people off and I don't get danger pay."

CANADIEN **TRENT MCCLEARY**

"We know he is a one-dimensional player, but it's the dimension we don't have."

CALGARY FLAMES GM **AL COATES**, ON PHIL HOUSLEY

"I have 3,000 penalty minutes. I don't need people dictating to me how to do my job."

MAPLE LEAF **TIE DOMI**, ON FAN AND MEDIA CRITICISM

"We had too many guys hurt their arms patting themselves on the back. Now, they're probably rubbing their feet from being sore kicking themselves."

COYOTES COACH **JIM SCHOENFELD**, AFTER BLOWING A 4-1 LEAD AND LOSING TO TORONTO

"It would have been worse if we hadn't blocked the kick after Toronto's second touchdown."

RED WING **ALEX DELVECCHIO**, AFTER TORONTO BEAT DETROIT 13-0 IN 1971

"Not if they check the date on the ticket. That wasn't entertainment."

ST. LOUIS BLUE **TONY TWIST**, AFTER BEING TOLD THAT THE COST OF TICKETS
TO A 4-0 ST. LOUIS WIN OVER TORONTO COULD BE WRITTEN OFF ON INCOME TAXES
AS AN ENTERTAINMENT DEDUCTION

137

"He's going down like free beer at a frat party."

CAPITALS GM PIERRE MCGUIRE, ON ISLANDER
MARIUSZ CZERKAWSKI'S FREQUENT DIVING

"My old man used to tell me, 'If you ain't dead, don't lay there.' Maybe a lot of guys didn't have fathers telling them that."

OILERS GM KEVIN LOWE, ON PLAYERS WHO FAKE INJURY TO DRAW A PENALTY

"Ah, my sister used to hit me harder."

RED WING SHAWN BURR, ON BEING CHECKED BY DALLAS STAR MIKE MODANO

"Let's put it this way: if one of my brothers were standing in front of the bus last night and we were about to leave and he was on the other team, I'd have run over him. I wouldn't have called out first to ask him to get out of the way, either. That's my mentality, that's the way it is. I don't really care."

BLACKHAWKS COACH BRIAN SUTTER, DURING A CHICAGO-ST. LOUIS PLAYOFF SERIES

"He could deke a guy in a phone booth."

SHARK OWEN NOLAN, ON TEAMMATE VIKTOR KOZLOV

"How you can have a guy who is [so small] dominate a hockey game like he does? He's mastered the art of being able to just stop and turn on a dime and avoid the monsters who are chasing him."

FLYER JEREMY ROENICK, ON PREDATOR CLIFF RONNING,
WHO HAD JUST PLAYED IN HIS 1,000TH NHL GAME

"Great lines in hockey could turn the lights off and know where each other is."

COYOTES GM MIKE BARNETT,
ON COYOTES TONY AMONTE AND DANNY BRIERE

"I know my players don't like my practices, but that's O.K. because I don't like their games."

CANUCKS COACH HARRY NEALE

"You can't play hockey if you're nice."

LIGHTNING COACH STEVE LUDZIK

"Maybe one of the qualities of being a great coach is being a Jerk. There are quite a few of them around."

L.A. KINGS COACH LARRY ROBINSON

"Coaches are like ducks.
Calm on top but paddling underneath. Believe me, there's a lot of leg movement."

DALLAS STARS COACH KEN HITCHCOCK, ON HIDING HIS NERVOUSNESS

"This is my third time. They say you're not a coach in the league till you've been fired. I must be getting pretty good."

WINNIPEG JETS COACH TERRY SIMPSON, AFTER BEING FIRED

"You can't keep on trading foot soldiers. Sooner or later, the general's got to go."

MAPLE LEAF COACH PAT BURNS, AFTER BEING FIRED BY TORONTO

"People don't remember records. They remember milestones."

LIGHTNING DAVE ANDREYCHUK, ONE GOAL AWAY FROM TYING PHIL ESPOSITO'S RECORD 249 POWER-PLAY GOALS, ON WHY HE'D RATHER SCORE HIS 600TH

"All that means is that I'll be 783 years old when I catch Scotty Bowman."

PENGUINS COACH KEVIN CONSTANTINE, AFTER BEING CONGRATULATED ON HIS 100TH CAREER WIN

"If I'd known it was going to take 25 years, I'd have started earlier."

DALLAS STAR COACH KEN HITCHCOCK, ON HOW LONG IT TOOK HIM TO GET TO THE STANLEY CUP FINALS

"So my decision, after 16 years, was to walk away now, rather than crawl away later."

HALL OF FAME NHL PLAYER DALE HAWERCHUK, ON HIS REASON TO RETIRE

"Man is that guy ripped. I mean, I've got the washboard stomach, too. It's just that mine has about two months of laundry on top of it."

SHARK SHAWN BURR, ON FLYER ERIC LINDROS

"I never thought I'd be an old, fat, ex-hockey player, but I became one."

MAPLE LEAFS GM AND COACH PAT QUINN

"It must be the body. It's chiseled out of marshmallows."

BLACKHAWK **TONY AMONTE**, ON POSSESSING THE NHL'S SECOND-LONGEST
ACTIVE PLAYING STREAK

"Players today put too much emphasis on lifting weights,
low body fat and big muscles that they think make them
look good — all that bullshit. What you need to play hockey
is heart and determination, and the ability to stay mentally
strong. Mental strength beats physical strength any day."

HALL OF FAME NHL PLAYER **PHIL ESPOSITO**, IN A 2003 INTERVIEW

"They always try to play with our minds. But that won't
work with our club. We've got 20 guys without brains."

FLYER **BOBBY CLARKE**, IN 1976, WHEN THE RUSSIAN CENTRAL ARMY TEAM
PLAYED PHILADELPHIA

"There's a thousand theories, but theories are for scientists.
We're too stupid for that. We've just got to get back to the
x's and o's."

SHARK **MIKE RICCI**, ON SAN JOSE'S SLOW START

"I see you finally got a number to match your IQ."

OILERS ASSISTANT COACH **BOB MCCAMMON**, TO MARTY MCSORLEY,
WHO WAS WEARING NUMBER 5

"You can always get someone to do your thinking for you."

HALL OF FAME RED WING **GORDIE HOWE**, DURING A 1970S APPEARANCE
ON "THE DICK CAVETT SHOW," ON WHY HOCKEY PLAYERS ALWAYS WEAR A PROTECTIVE CUP
BUT RARELY A HELMET

"Every time I see you naked, I feel sorry for your wife."

PENGUIN JAROMIR JAGR,
TO TEAMMATE MATTHEW BARNABY

"Everything was set for us to play a real good game. Then we left the dressing room and everything went to hell."

THRASHERS COACH CURT FRASER

"The playoffs separate the men from the boys, and we found out we have a lot of boys in our dressing room."

RANGERS GM NEIL SMITH, AFTER THE RANGERS LOST IN THE PLAYOFFS TO WASHINGTON

"I like to space them out so I can remember them."

FLYER CHRIS MCALLISTER, AFTER SCORING HIS FIRST GOAL IN 94 GAMES

"There's no reason why a player is done at 33, 34. They train better, they eat better, they drink better. This isn't the old days when everybody sat around and drank beer."

FLYERS GM BOB CLARKE, ON SIGNING 37-YEAR-OLD KJELL SAMUELSSON

"Usually, I'm on the bus by now, having a beer and waiting for everyone else. This is cutting into my beer time."

CAPITAL CRAIG BERUBE, TO THE MEDIA, AFTER SCORING ONE OF HIS RARE GOALS
AND BEING THE CENTER OF ATTENTION IN THE DRESSING ROOM

"Bud Light."

ST. LOUIS BLUE KEITH TKACHUK, ASKED TO NAME HIS FAVORITE SPORTS DRINK
IN THE TEAM MEDIA GUIDE

"If you're looking for the guy we got for Marty, he'll be here in four years."

MIGHTY DUCK STEVE SHIELDS, BITTER AFTER TEAMMATE MARTY MCINNIS
WENT TO BOSTON FOR A DRAFT PICK

"I'll be sad to go and I wouldn't be sad to go. It wouldn't upset me to leave St. Louis, but it would upset me to leave St. Louis. It's hard to explain. You'll find out one of these days, but maybe you never will."

ST. LOUIS BLUE BRETT HULL, ON A POSSIBLE TRADE

"It's not so much maturity as it is growing up."

BRUIN JAY MILLER, ASKED IF HIS IMPROVED PLAY WAS DUE TO MATURITY

"I love to play for Pittsburgh. If they can't afford me, then I'd love to play in L.A. or New York."

PENGUIN JAROMIR JAGR

"Yeah, I'm cocky and I am arrogant. But that doesn't mean I'm not a nice person."

COYOTE JEREMY ROENICK

"Guys, I don't want to tell you half-truths, unless they're completely accurate. "

CANADIENS COACH ALAIN VIGNEAULT, AFTER A LOSS IN 1999

"We get nose jobs all the time in the NHL, and we don't even have to go to the hospital."

HALL OF FAME BRUIN **BRAD PARK**

I knew I was in trouble when I heard
snap, crackle and pop,
and I wasn't having a bowl of cereal.

MAPLE LEAF NICK KYPREOS, AFTER SUFFERING A SPIRAL ANKLE FRACTURE IN A FIGHT

"I just tape four Tylenols to it."

OILER **BORIS MIRONOV**, ON PLAYING WITH A SORE ANKLE

"It's no big deal. Like Gordie Howe says, elbows are to hockey players what fenders are to cars."

CANADIAN **ERIC LINDROS**, ON HAVING HIS ELBOW DRAINED DURING THE 1996 WORLD CUP

"I think I might get 1,000 stitches before I get to 1,000 points."

COYOTE **JEREMY ROENICK**, AFTER TAKING A GASH TO THE FACE

"I was kind of hoping it would straighten it out. One of these times it will."

FLYER **ROD BRIND'AMOUR**, AFTER SUFFERING HIS FOURTH BROKEN NOSE

"Biologically,
I'm 10.
Chronologically,
I'm 33.
In hockey years,
I'm 66."

RANGER MARK MESSIER

"I've never had major knee surgery on any other part of my body."

CANADIEN **SAKU KOIVU**, TO REPORTERS

"I'm convinced the head goes before the body. You end up not wanting to pay the price. It happens to every athlete eventually. In a physical contact sport, it shows up quicker. A guy gets tired of hitting or being hit. You can't hide that once it happens."

NHL PLAYER, COACH AND GM BOBBY CLARKE

"I had a poster of Probert on my wall. When I fought him for the first and only time, I thought to myself, 'Great, I got out alive.'"

ISLANDER ERIC CAIRNS, ON HIS CHILDHOOD IDOL BOB PROBERT

"It's not who wins the fight that's important, it's being willing to fight. If you get challenged and renege, everyone wants to take a shot at you."

NHL PLAYER AND COACH BARCLAY PLAGER

"Two people fighting is not violence in hockey. It might be in tennis or bowling, but it's not in hockey."

NHL GOALIE AND COACH GERRY CHEEVERS

"Lemieux fights like a girl. He couldn't beat his way out of a paper bag."

RANGERS COACH JOHN MUCKLER, ON NJ DEVIL CLAUDE LEMIEUX

"We're scared of losing. That's why we win. We know what it's like to lose and we hate it. We enjoy being champions too much."

ISLANDER BOB BOURNE, ON HIS TEAM'S FOUR STANLEY CUP WINS IN THE 1980S

"Potential is synonymous with getting your ass kicked."

PENGUINS COACH KEVIN CONSTANTINE, ASKED IF HIS TEAM HAD POTENTIAL

"It's the nuts and bolts time of the year and we don't have enough nuts and bolts."

SHARKS COACH DARRYL SUTTER, ON A LATE-SEASON LOSING STREAK

"When we think he has run out of incredible things to do, he does something incredible again. You wonder how much better the kid can get."

PENGUINS COACH KEVIN CONSTANTINE, ON JAROMIR JAGR

"The only way we could have, was to have shot him before the game started."

CALGARY FLAMES COACH BRIAN SUTTER,
ON HOW HIS TEAM COULD HAVE STOPPED JAROMIR JAGR

"If you play him like a regular guy, he will bury you."

DEVILS GOALIE MARTIN BRODEUR

"There are probably four ways to play Jagr, all of them wrong. He's the toughest player in hockey to devise a game plan against."

BLUE JACKETS COACH **DAVE KING**

"We only speak two languages here: English and profanity."

PENGUINS COACH **KEVIN CONSTANTINE**, ON THE MANY NATIVE LANGUAGES SPOKEN BY HIS TEAM

"He brings something special. I don't know what it is, but if you ask him, you couldn't understand his answer."

RANGER **WAYNE GRETZKY**, ON ESA TIKKANEN

"He's one of those guys whose English gets worse every year. But as long as it doesn't affect his play, we're all right."

MAPLE LEAF **WADE BELAK**, ON CZECH TEAMMATE TOMAS KABERLE'S THICK ACCENT

"They do a lot of talking, but I'm not sure they actually understand each other."

RED WING **DARREN MCCARTY**, ON TEAMMATE VLADIMIR KONSTANTINOV AND AVALANCHE CLAUDE LEMIEUX

"Hell, I don't know if he speaks French."

CANADIENS COACH **TOE BLAKE**, WHEN ASKED IF QUIET ROOKIE HENRI RICHARD SPOKE ANY ENGLISH

153

"Only in America."

"Most people have friends, but no money. I have the
opposite. I don't have a chance to talk to my real friends,
the ones I've had since I was five years old. Sometimes
I wish I could bring Czechoslovakia to America. Then
I would be the happiest guy in the world."

PENGUIN **JAROMIR JAGR**

"To get my paycheque for two weeks, my family must work
200 years in Slovakia."

ST. LOUIS BLUE **PAVOL DEMITRA**, ON HIS $1.1-MILLION SALARY

"The only pressure I'm under is the pressure I've put on myself."

RANGER MARK MESSIER

"When he gets mad, it's like he's in another world. He'll look at you with those big eyes and they'll be going around in circles."

RETIRED (1990) RANGER BARRY BECK, ON MARK MESSIER

"He ran over a few people, nothing major. Mess runs over people. Sometimes, people don't get up. That's life."

HALL OF FAME NHL GOALIE GRANT FUHR, ON MARK MESSIER

"It's much easier to slow down a thoroughbred than have to kick a donkey to get him going."

THRASHERS COACH BOB HARTLEY, ON NOT WANTING TO REIN IN SNIPER ILYA KOVALCHUK TOO MUCH

"For the most part, with the possible exception of me, I don't think anybody goes out to try to hurt somebody."

FLYER JEREMY ROENICK

"Dirty isn't a derogatory word. It's a good thing to be in hockey."

RED WING STEVE YZERMAN, ASKED ABOUT CAPITAL DALE HUNTER'S STYLE

"**Most people** who **don't** know I **play** hockey **think** I was **thrown** through a plate-glass **window** or something."

CALGARY FLAME **THEO FLEURY**,
ON THE 500 STITCHES HE HAS RECEIVED IN HIS CAREER

"Wayne came over to the bench one day after seeing Chara, and said, 'That's why I'm quitting.'"

RANGER COACH JOHN MUCKLER, LAUGHING ABOUT WAYNE GRETZKY'S COMMENT ON OTTAWA'S SIX-FOOT-NINE DEFENSEMAN ZDENO CHARA

"I looked like a big stiff [on television]. What a sobering experience. I always thought of myself as Nureyev on ice. But on TV, I realized that I was a dump truck. I was a elephant on wheels."

HALL OF FAME CANADIENS GOALIE KEN DRYDEN

"I'm not dirty, just aggressive. Fighter pilots have machine guns. I have only my mask and stick."

BRUINS GOALIE GERRY CHEEVERS

"I play a position where you make mistakes. The only people who don't make them at a hockey game are the ones watching."

AVALANCHE GOALIE PATRICK ROY

"With goaltenders, when they are on, the pucks look like beach balls. When they are a little bit off, they look like BBs."

PREDATORS COACH BARRY TROTZ

"Yeah, the two that went in."

BRUINS GOALIE GERRY CHEEVERS, ASKED IF HE COULD REMEMBER ANY SHOTS THAT WERE PARTICULARLY DIFFICULT TO HANDLE IN A 2-2 TIE AGAINST PHILADELPHIA

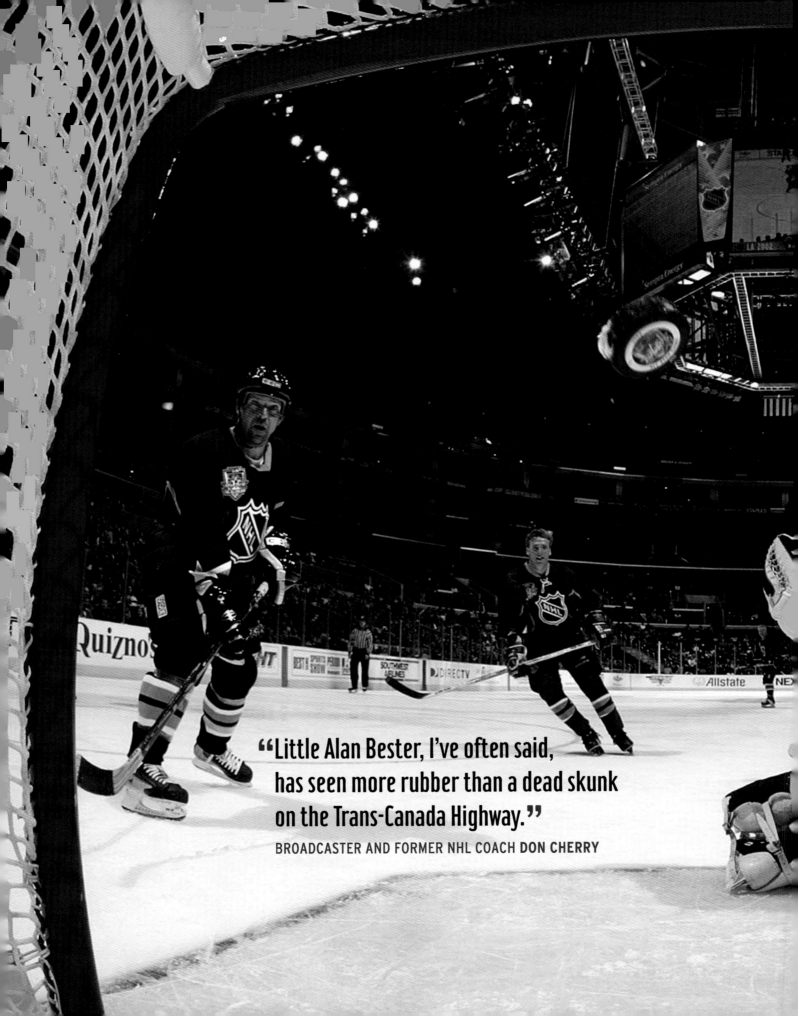

"Little Alan Bester, I've often said, has seen more rubber than a dead skunk on the Trans-Canada Highway."

BROADCASTER AND FORMER NHL COACH **DON CHERRY**

"Rocket had that mean look on, every game we played. He was 100 percent hockey. He could hate with the best of them."

HALL OF FAME RED WING GORDIE HOWE, ON MAURICE RICHARD

"It's still a bit blurry but I can see. I can tell what color the jerseys are."

PANTHER DAVE GAGNER, ON GETTING HIT IN THE EYE WITH A PUCK DURING WARM-UP

"It's nice to get a standing ovation in Montreal."

PANTHER SCOTT MELLANBY, WHO WAS KNOCKED UNCONSCIOUS AFTER SLIDING AND HITTING THE BACK OF HIS HEAD ON THE BOARDS, ON THE APPLAUSE HE RECEIVED AS HE WAS CARRIED OFF THE ICE ON A STRETCHER

"I didn't drop my gloves. They were yanked off me."

DALLAS STAR MIKE MODANO, ON HIS 1997 FIGHT WITH OILER KELLY BUCHBERGER

"We know that hockey is where we live, where we can best meet and overcome pain and wrong and death. Life is just a place where we spend time between games."

FLYERS COACH FRED SHERO

"How's the game changed in my 15 years in the league? Well, we used to be called hard-working players. Now we're overpaid crybabies."

RED WING BRETT HULL

"It's like the animal kingdom. Adapt or go extinct."

RED WING BRETT HULL, ON ADJUSTING HIS STYLE WHILE CONTINUING TO SCORE GOALS

"I am 10 times smarter than everyone else in this game. Beyond a shadow of a doubt."

RED WING BRETT HULL

"Hullie's a lot like a garbage can. You step on the pedal with your foot and the top opens up."

ST. LOUIS BLUE WAYNE GRETZKY, ON TEAMMATE BRETT HULL'S FREQUENTLY CONTROVERSIAL QUOTES

"A.m. or p.m.?"

CANADA'S STEVE YZERMAN, RESPONDING TO 1998 TEAM USA OLYMPIAN HULL'S CLAIM THAT "EIGHT NIGHTS OUT OF TEN, I WAS IN BED BY EIGHT."

"I wouldn't urinate in his ear if his brain was on fire."

HALL OF FAME BLACKHAWK BOBBY HULL, ON A LONGTIME MONTREAL RIVAL

I'M THE LUCKIEST MAN ALIVE. I DON'T EVEN LIKE THE GAME AND I'M SUCCESSFUL AT IT.

ST. LOUIS BLUE

"Fifty percent of the game is mental and the other fifty percent is being mental. I've got that part down, no problem."

ST. LOUIS BLUE BASIL MCRAE

"I remember my first year, I hit him with three good punches and couldn't believe he was still standing. He hit me with one and cracked my helmet. My head hurt for a week."

OILER GEORGES LARAQUE, ON STU GRIMSON

"All my friends back home fight on the street, and all they get is arrested."

PREDATOR PATRICK COTE, ON HIS $375,000 SALARY, MOSTLY EARNED AS A FIGHTER

"I'd rather fight than score."

FLYER DAVE "THE HAMMER" SCHULTZ

"There is no such thing as painless goaltending. If they could get enough padding to assure against every type of bruise, you'd have to be swung into position with a small derrick."

DON CHERRY

"I don't mind [Pavel] Bure or [Alexei] Yashin. I don't mind Markus Naslund. But if you get Europeans who don't score, they're useless, because they don't do anything else."

DON CHERRY

"The people who yell and scream about **hockey violence** are a handful of **intellectuals** and **newspapermen** who **never pay** to get in to see a game. The **fans,** who **shell out** the money, have always liked **good, rough hockey."**

DON CHERRY

"They don't know a lick about hockey. They never leave in the third period because they think there's a fourth one."

PREDATOR **TOM FITZGERALD**, ON NASHVILLE FANS

"The worst thing you can do is overreact. But it's also not good to underreact either."

DEVILS GM **LOU LAMORIELLO**, AFTER THE DEFENDING STANLEY CUP CHAMPIONS
FAILED TO MAKE THE PLAYOFFS

"Ranger fans are the rudest and they're proud of it, I'm sure."

BRUIN **BYRON DAFOE**

"He could rile up the Montreal fans in a hurry. God, sometimes I felt sorry for the man. He must have got a standing ovation when he went shopping."

HALL OF FAME RED WING **GORDIE HOWE**, ON MAURICE RICHARD

"We're giving the fans their money's worth. We're super-sizing the games for them."

PANTHER **PETER WORRELL**, ON FLORIDA'S 13 OVERTIME GAMES
BY MIDWAY THROUGH THE SEASON

"I'm just glad it wasn't Machete Night."

RANGER **BOB FROESE**, AFTER FANS THREW PLASTIC MUGS ONTO THE ICE ON MUG NIGHT

"We appreciate all the fans that are here, but we really respect the five or six who stayed with us all year."

NORTH STAR **JON CASEY**, ON MAKING THE PLAYOFFS

"We're not sharp on the bench. I know I get screwed up sometimes going left to right but if you can count to five that's the main thing. We've got a few who have a problem."

CANUCK **MARKUS NASLUND**, ON VANCOUVER'S LEAGUE-LEADING NUMBER
OF BENCH MINORS FOR TOO MANY MEN ON THE ICE

"It's going to be nice to be embarrassed in practice instead of games."

PANTHER **RHETT WARRENER**, ON HAVING PAVEL BURE BECOME A TEAMMATE

"If I had the answers to all those things, I wouldn't be a fourth-line left winger."

PENGUIN **STEVE MCKENNA**, A FORMER RANGER, ASKED HOW HIS TEAM WON
WHEN THE RANGERS WERE IN A DESPERATE STRUGGLE TO MAKE THE 2003 PLAYOFFS

"The scum of the league really came through tonight."

MAPLE LEAF **ALYN MCCAULEY**, AFTER HE, TIE DOMI AND JYRKI LUMME SCORED
IN TORONTO'S 3-1 WIN OVER CHICAGO

"Even a blind dog finds a bone once in a while."

ST. LOUIS BLUE **KELLY CHASE**, AFTER THE ENFORCER SCORED TWICE IN 33 SECONDS
AND ADDED AN ASSIST IN A 5-1 WIN AGAINST PREDATORS

"Being called a frog 20 times a day is something that ends up getting on your nerves."

RED WING MARTIN LAPOINTE, ON AN ARGUMENT AND FIGHT HE HAD WITH HIS TEAM CANADA
TEAMMATE ERIC LINDROS BEFORE THE 1991 JUNIOR WORLD CHAMPIONSHIP

"I think our players need to pick themselves up off the floor and get going. It's time for them to stop feeling nervous and feeling sorry for themselves, and time to go out and play. You play hard, you'll enjoy it. If you enjoy it, you're winning."

COYOTES MANAGING PARTNER **WAYNE GRETZKY**,
ON THE COYOTES' POOR FIRST HALF OF THE 2002-03 SEASON

"I score most of my goals in the third period because I don't like to lose."

ISLANDER **MARK PARRISH**

"Winning does solve everything."

AVALANCHE **JOE SAKIC**

"If you're built like a freight train, you can't drive around like a Volkswagen."

HALL OF FAME ISLANDER **CLARK GILLIES**,

ON UNDERACHIEVING ISLANDER TODD BERTUZZI

"Where are you putting the penalty box?"

MAPLE LEAF **TIE DOMI**, ASKING HIS FIRST QUESTION DURING HIS TOUR
OF THE AIR CANADA CENTRE UNDER CONSTRUCTION

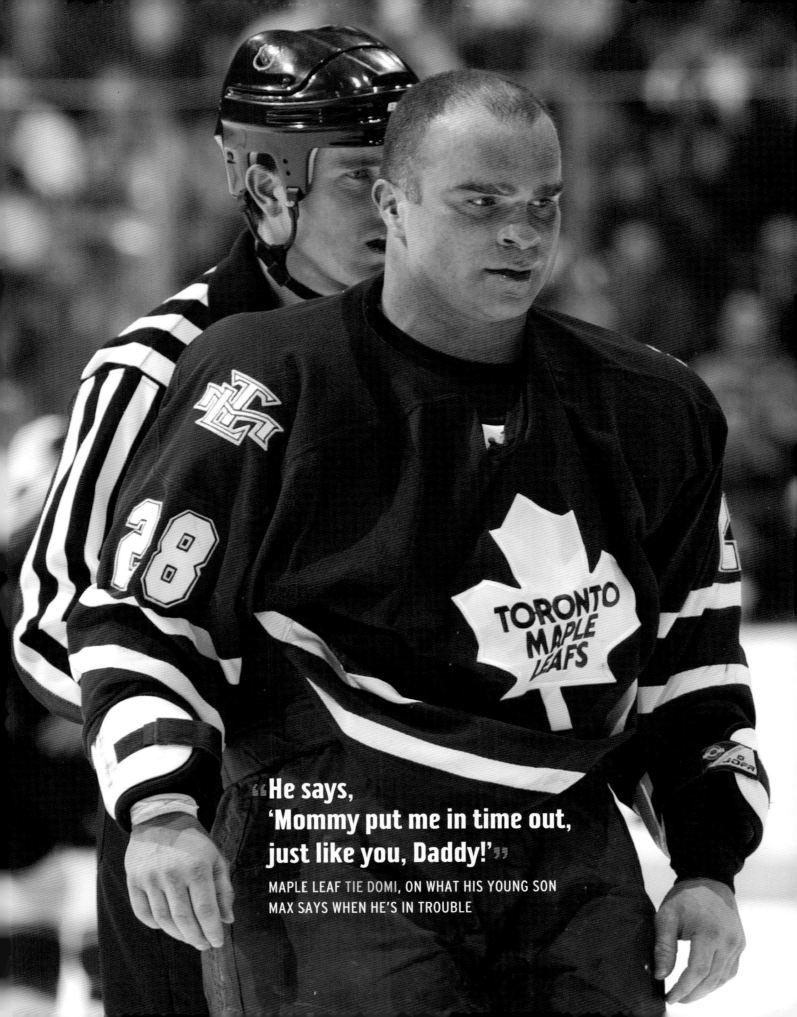

"He says,
'Mommy put me in time out,
just like you, Daddy!'"

MAPLE LEAF TIE DOMI, ON WHAT HIS YOUNG SON
MAX SAYS WHEN HE'S IN TROUBLE

"She looks like her mother, thank God."

WINNIPEG JET TIE DOMI, ON HIS BABY DAUGHTER

"His eyes are wide open and he looks alert. He might be a goalie."

MIGHTY DUCKS GOALIE DOMINIC ROUSSEL, ON THE BIRTH OF HIS BABY BOY

"Daddy, you're the best hockey player in the world except that you can't score."

CLANCY WILLIAMS, SIX-YEAR-OLD DAUGHTER OF CANUCK DAVE "TIGER" WILLIAMS, DURING A SCORING SLUMP

"I'd have to answer to my mom."

PANTHER ROB NIEDERMAYER, ON WHAT WOULD HAPPEN IF HE BOARDED HIS BROTHER SCOTT

"I told her they must all be sold out."

MAPLE LEAF WADE BELAK, ON HIS RESPONSE WHEN HIS MOTHER SAID SHE COULDN'T FIND HIS SWEATER FOR SALE AT THE AIR CANADA CENTRE'S SOUVENIR SHOP

"My mom, she keeps telling me she wants a goal. I tell her: 'Hey Mom, I'm tryin', I'm tryin', every day.'"

BRUIN PJ STOCK

"Lunch is on me."

RED WING BRENDAN SHANAHAN, AFTER SIGNING A $26-MILLION CONTRACT

"I would cry a lot, so I try not to think about it."

HALL OF FAME PLAYER BRAD PARK, ASKED WHAT HE WOULD EARN IN TODAY'S GAME

"Bert's wallet is like an onion. Any time he opens it, he starts crying."

CANUCK BRENDAN MORRISON, ON TEAMMATE TODD BERTUZZI

"I never knew the rules. I used common sense. It's really the only way to run a game. If officials called every penalty they saw, there would be no players on the ice and no one in the rink."

HALL OF FAME NHL REFEREE BILL CHADWICK

"It's the first time a ref ever listened to me."

MIGHTY DUCKS GOALIE GUY HEBERT, AFTER REFEREE DAN MAROUELLI TOOK HIS REQUEST, WENT FOR VIDEO REVIEW AND DENIED A GOAL

"First they give him two, then it's five, then a game [misconduct]. I was wondering whether the electric chair was next."

HURRICANES COACH PAUL MAURICE, ON ERIK COLE'S HIT ON OTTAWA'S CHRIS PHILLIPS

"I was so excited. I was 26 and I didn't think I was ever going to make it to the NHL. I forgot that I was there to stop pucks."

RANGER ED GIACOMIN, ON HIS DISAPPOINTING 1965-66 ROOKIE SEASON

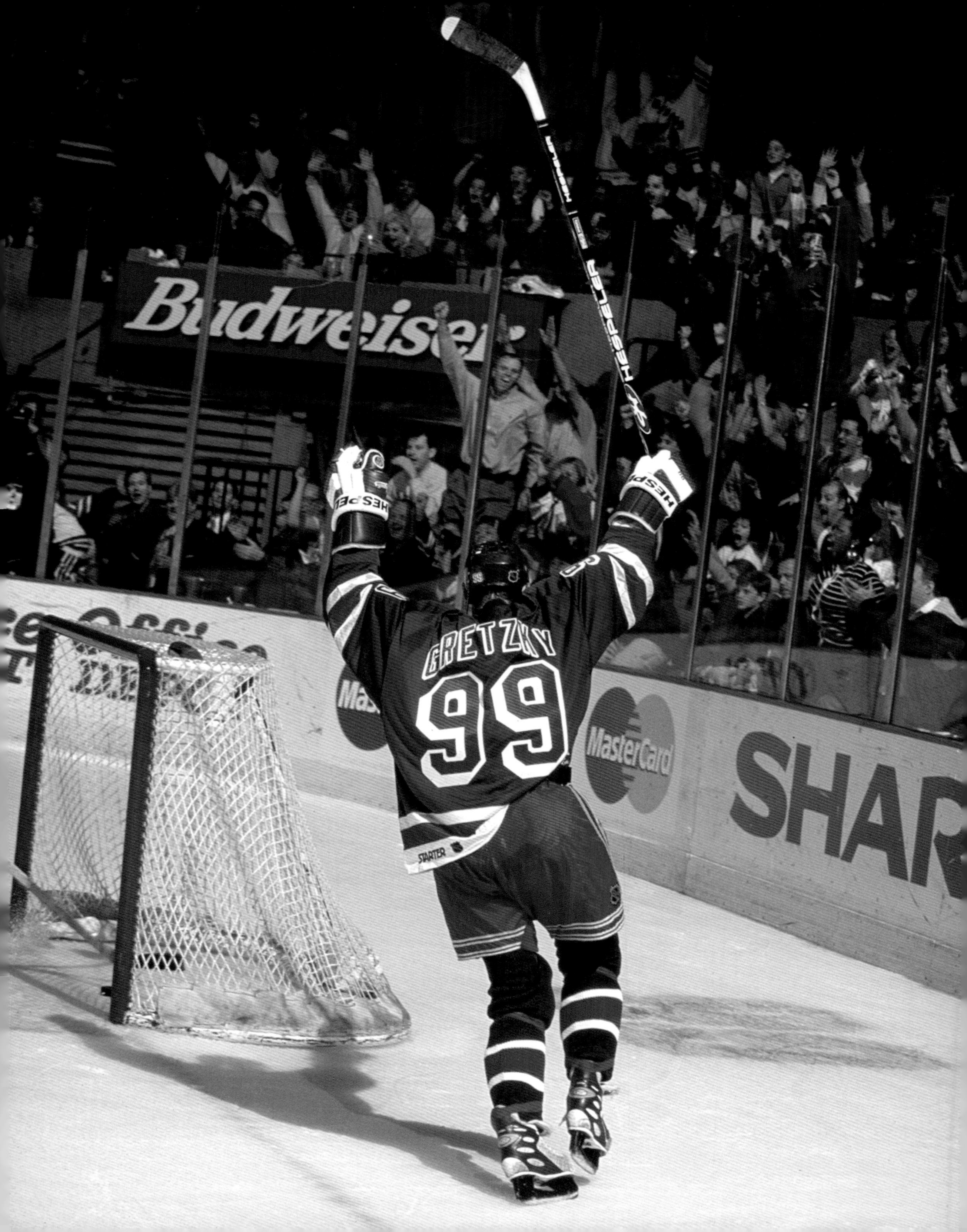
Budweiser
HESPELER
GRETZKY
99
MasterCard
STARTER

"The hardest thing for me has always been that I've been compared to myself."

RANGER WAYNE GRETZKY

"I can't hear what Jeremy says because my ears are blocked with my two Stanley Cup rings."

AVALANCHE **PATRICK ROY**, RESPONDING TO A REMARK FROM BLACKHAWK JEREMY ROENICK

"Some nights, I'd like to shoot some of them myself."

RANGERS PRESIDENT **NEIL SMITH**, RESPONDING TO FASHION PHOTOGRAPHER BRUCE WEBER'S STATEMENT THAT HE WOULD LIKE TO SHOOT SOME OF THE RANGERS

"Every time a puck gets past me and I look back in my net, I say 'Oh, oh.'"

FLYER GOALIE **BERNIE PARENT**, ON WHY HE CHOSE NUMBER OO IN THE WHA

"Oh, yes, I love sleepless nights."

L.A. KINGS COACH **LARRY ROBINSON**, ON WHETHER HE PLANNED TO RETURN TO COACH THE TEAM THE FOLLOWING SEASON

"Sure, Daniel wears number 22 and Henrik number 33."

CANUCKS COACH **MARC CRAWFORD**, ON WHETHER HE COULD TELL THE SEDIN TWINS APART

"You'll never catch me bragging about goals, but I'll talk all you want about my assists."

OILER **WAYNE GRETZKY**

"Some people skate to the puck. I skate to where the puck is going to be."

L.A. KING **WAYNE GRETZKY**

"It's a special feeling, a great thrill. I owe everything I have in my life to hockey and the NHL. The game doesn't owe me anything. So, something like this is very special."

RANGER WAYNE GRETZKY AFTER HIS NUMBER 99 WAS OFFICIALLY RETIRED

"There should be a league rule where he is passed around from team to team each year."

BRUINS COACH TERRY O'REILLY, AFTER GRETZKY HELPED EDMONTON SWEEP THE BRUINS IN THE 1988 STANLEY CUP FINALS

"The only way you can check Gretzky is to hit him when he is standing still singing the national anthem."

BRUINS GM HARRY SINDEN

"If Jaromir Jagr can wear a mullet for eight years, why can't I wear a Mohawk?"

MAPLE LEAF BRYAN MCCABE, ON CRITICISM OVER HIS NEW HAIRSTYLE

"Anybody I can't stand to play against, I would like to play with."

FLYER ERIC LINDROS, ON PLAYING WITH CLAUDE LEMIEUX AND BRENDAN SHANAHAN FOR TEAM CANADA

"Jason Arnott will be here as long as I'm here, for the time being."

OILERS GM GLEN SATHER, ON JASON ARNOTT TRADE RUMORS

"What I've learned so far from researching is that to win the Stanley Cup, you have to make the playoffs."

CAPITALS OWNER TED LEONSIS

"The first thing I noticed about him was that he was born the same year I was drafted. That's a pretty scary thought."

ST. LOUIS BLUE AL MACINNIS, AT AGE 36, ON A 1999 ROOKIE TEAMMATE

"I'm trying to act like every other guy, but inside there is a party going on."

AVALANCHE JEFF DAW, ON BEING CALLED UP BY COLORADO FOR HIS FIRST NHL GAME
AFTER FIVE-AND-A-HALF YEARS IN THE MINORS

"I look out there during the warm-ups and I see Brett Hull and Niklas Lidstrom and Brendan Shanahan and Sergei Fedorov. I'm used to playing these guys in video games and here I am about to play against them for real. It was a dream come true."

MINNESOTA WILD STEPHANE VEILLEUX, ON MAKING HIS NHL DEBUT AGAINST DETROIT

"The Cold War is back on."

SENATOR SHAWN MCEACHERN, ON TEAMMATE ALEXEI YASHIN'S AGENT CLAIMING BIGOTRY

"I'm not crazy, I'm Russian."

MAPLE LEAF DIMITRI YUSHKEVICH

"This is definitely the best team I have played [on] in the National Hockey League, but in Russia, the teams I played for were some of the best teams in the history of the game."

RED WING IGOR LARIONOV, WHO PLAYED FOR RUSSIAN OLYMPIC AND WORLD CHAMPIONSHIP
GOLD MEDAL TEAMS

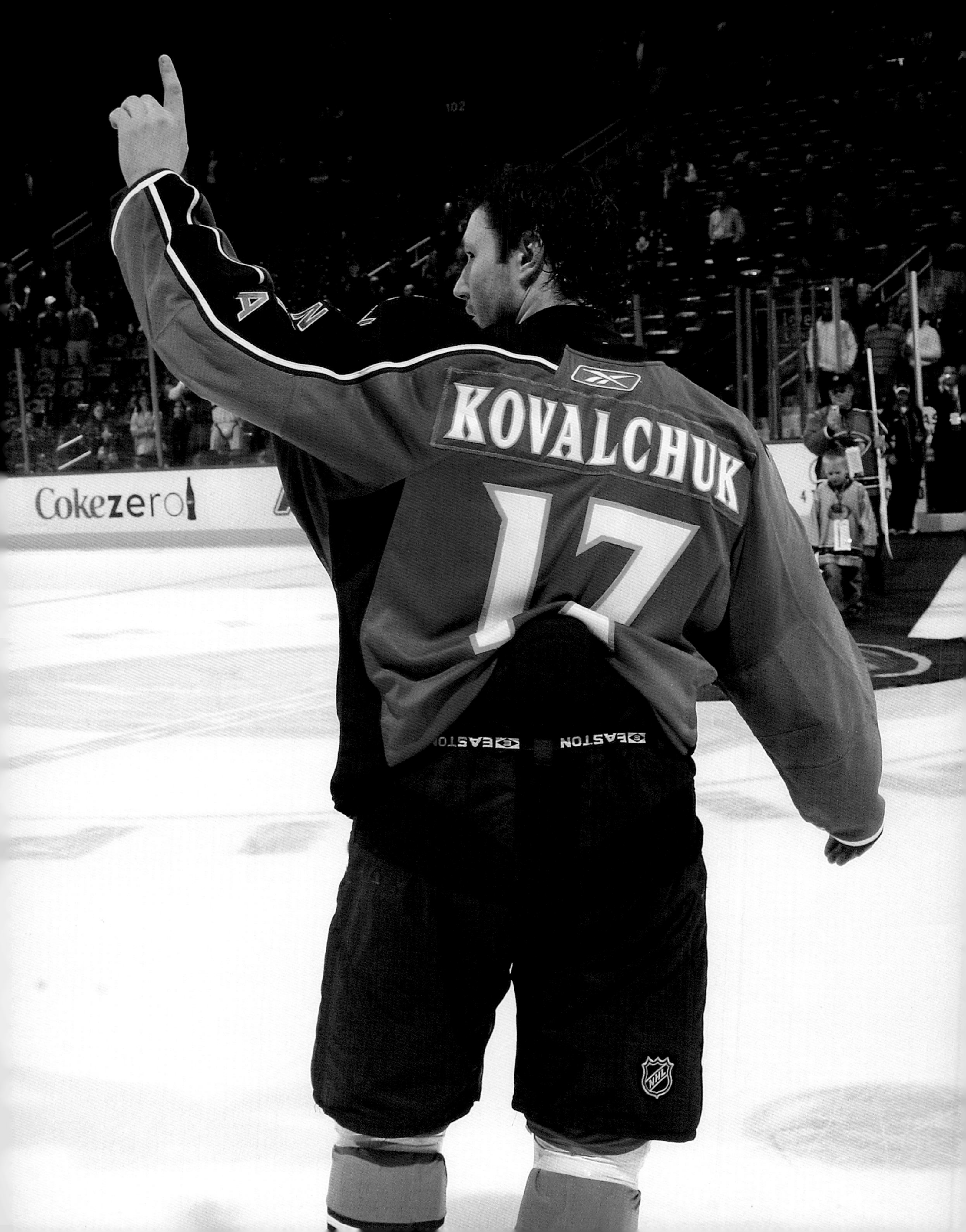
KOVALCHUK
17
Cokezero
EASTON
EASTON

"THEY SAY SOMETHING TO ME SOMETIMES. BUT I DON'T UNDERSTAND ALL THE WORDS YET. SO I SMILE AT THEM AND THEN I SCORE A GOAL."

THRASHER , ASKED IF HE GETS VERBALLY ABUSED
BY OPPONENTS ON THE ICE

"I've always felt hockey was like a disease. You can't really shake it."

CALGARY FLAMES GOALIE KEN WREGGET

"Hockey is a man's game. The team with the most real men wins."

CANUCKS GM BRIAN BURKE

"You have to know what pro hockey is all about. You have to live and breathe and sleep it. You have to lose a few teeth and take some shots to the face. It's not a pretty thing."

SABRES COACH TED NOLAN

"Hockey is like a religion in Montreal. You're either a saint or a sinner, there's no in-between."

AVALANCHE AND FORMER CANADIENS GOALIE PATRICK ROY

"Our dreams and thoughts were always to one day lift this trophy. When you do it's a fact and no one can ever take that away from you."

OILER WAYNE GRETZKY

"If we do win this thing, that Cup's going to be beside me at the altar. I hope the wife doesn't get too mad."

CAPITAL OLAF KOLZIG, ON HIS UPCOMING WEDDING

182

"I'd rather tame a tiger than paint stripes on a kitty cat."

SHARKS GM DEAN LOMBARDI, ON OBTAINING FREQUENTLY SUSPENDED BRYAN MARCHMENT

"A complacent player is a lazy player, and a lazy player is a loser."

BLACKHAWKS COACH DARRYL SUTTER

"I don't order fries with my club sandwich."

PENGUIN MARIO LEMIEUX, TO TEAMMATE RON FRANCIS,
WHO ASKED HIM WHAT HE DID TO STAY IN SHAPE IN THE OFF-SEASON

"One thing I hate is people screaming at me. If you want me to do something, talk to me. When someone screams at me to hurry up, I slow down."

PENGUIN MARIO LEMIEUX

"Usually when you play a team, you want to focus on one line. Pittsburgh is the only team where you have to focus on one player. When he's coming toward you, all you see is him."

CANADIENS GOALIE PATRICK ROY

"There's no book on Mario. It's not like he has a favorite thing that he does over and over. Every time it's a different adventure. And you know that if he does the things that he wants to do, the puck's going to go in the net."

WHALERS GOALIE PETER SIDORKIEWICZ

"His face is so calm.
He shows no signs of stress or anything.
It's as if he's saying,

'No problem. Relax. I'm just going to beat
you now. It's not going to hurt a bit.' "

FLYERS GOALIE DOMINIC ROUSSEL ABOUT PENGUIN MARIO LEMIEUX

"There is no position in sport as noble as goaltending."

HALL OF FAME SOVIET UNION NATIONAL TEAM GOALIE VLADISLAV TRETIAK

"Playing with Steve Guolla is like playing with myself."

SHARK JEFF FRIESEN, ON HIS TEAMMATE

"He's the kind of guy who will stab you in the back right to your face."

ST. LOUIS BLUE BRETT HULL, ON COACH MIKE KEENAN

"You hit the head right on the nail."

SABRE BRIAN HOLZINGER, DURING A FIRST INTERMISSION INTERVIEW

"Those were little monumental mistakes."

CANADIENS COACH JEAN PERRON

"That's a whole new ball of worms."

HURRICANE ROD BRIND'AMOUR, UPSET AFTER DOCTORS FOUND A SECOND BREAK
IN HIS LEFT FCOT

"Getting cut in the face is a pain in the butt."

CALGARY FLAME THEO FLEURY

"We have only one person to blame, and that's each other."

RANGER BARRY BECK, AFTER A LOSS

"Even our train found the injured list. It broke down going from Washington to Philadelphia this week. Typifies our season so far."

COYOTES GM MIKE BARNETT, ON HIS TEAM'S INJURY-RIDDLED CAMPAIGN

"The goal is too small and the goalies are too big."

RED WINGS COACH SCOTTY BOWMAN, ON WHY GOALS ARE HARD TO COME BY

"I'd be lying to you if I said guys weren't afraid of him. I'm afraid of him, afraid of him running into me."

PANTHER PAUL LAUS, ON SIX-FOOT-SIX TEAMMATE PETER WORRELL

"He's not big in size, but he's big in heart."

LIGHTNING ROB ZAMUNER, ON TEAMMATE DARCY TUCKER

"The bigger they are, the harder they hit."

BRUINS ASSISTANT-GM MIKE O'CONNELL, ON ACQUIRING SIX-FOOT-FOUR,
225-POUND KEN BELANGER IN 1998

"If I hadn't learned to lay on a two-hander once in a while, I'd never have left Flin Flon."

FLYER BOBBY CLARKE, IN 1972

"First time I've ever been this close to one without it being broken over my head."

RED WING DARREN MCCARTY, AFTER BLACKHAWK CHRIS CHELIOS GOT TRADED TO DETROIT,
AS HE STROLLED OVER TO THE STICK RACK AND GRABBED ONE OF CHELIOS'S STICKS

"I believe Bobby Orr had the greatest impact of any player to come along in my lifetime. He earned his place in hockey history by single handedly changing the game from the style played in my day. In my mind there can be no greater legacy."

HALL OF FAME CANADIEN **JEAN BELIVEAU**

"I don't think you ever stopped Bobby Orr. You contained Bobby Orr, but you never stopped him. When we played the Bruins and Bobby had to give up the puck, it was a good play."

HALL OF FAME CANADIEN **LARRY ROBINSON**

"If I can be half the hockey player that Bobby Orr was, I'll be happy."

BRUIN RAY BOURQUE

"I always tell Bobby he was up in the air for so long that I had time to shower and change before he hit the ice."

HALL OF FAME ST. LOUIS BLUES GOALIE **GLENN HALL**,
ON BOBBY ORR'S FAMOUS GOAL TO WIN THE 1970 STANLEY CUP

"Forget about style; worry about results"

HALL OF FAME BRUIN **BOBBY ORR**

"There are two things I don't want to know: how they make hot dogs and what goes on in the NHL office."

"They kept me in the dark and every once in a while opened the door and threw manure on me."

"One time I was told to go down the hall, past the picture of Cinderella, and turn left. Another time I was told to go upstairs and turn right when I saw Peter Pan."

"How about those quick face-offs this year? The owners can't be happy. Games are 20 minutes faster — hurts the concession sales."

"I don't want to be sitting back and watching other guys do everything."

"Yes, and I also like jumping out of tall buildings."

PANTHER JOHN VANBIESBROUCK, ASKED IF HE ENJOYED FACING 51 SHOTS IN A GAME

"I get pissed off sometimes when it seems like I couldn't get it into an ocean if I was on a beach."

FLAME DENIS GAUTHIER, ON HAVING HIS SHOTS BLOCKED

"Branko, you're not going to make a lot of money unless you shoot."

PHOENIX COACH BOBBY FRANCIS, TO COYOTE ROOKIE BRANKO RADIVOJEVIC

"Well, I've got my teeth right here in my hand."

CANUCK MIKE SILLINGER, TRYING TO PROVE TO REFEREE BILL MCCREARY THAT HE WAS CROSS-CHECKED BY MAPLE LEAF JAMIE MACOUN

"I was trying to hit him in the chest. Too bad I missed."

BLUE JACKET SERGE AUBIN, ON KNOCKING OUT TWO OF PENGUIN DARIUS KASPARAITIS'S TEETH

"I'd like to thank my parents for messing around 29 years ago."

RED WING MANNY LEGACE, AFTER WINNING THE STANLEY CUP

"Tell him he's Wayne Gretzky"

OILERS COACH **TED GREEN**, AFTER OILER SHAUN VAN ALLEN
SUFFERED A CONCUSSION AND COULDN'T REMEMBER WHO HE WAS.

"I was 14 when I lost them [his front teeth]. The main thing was, we won that game, so I was the happiest. You hate to lose your teeth and the game, too."

HALL OF FAME FLYER BILL BARBER

"Daneyko got mad when Kaminski said he was going to knock his teeth out. Dano has only two teeth left, so you can't say that to Dano."

DEVILS COACH JACQUES LEMAIRE, ON A FIGHT BETWEEN DEVIL KEN DANEYKO AND CAPITA_ KEVIN KAMINSKI

"He has a great body for a hockey player, too. I don't want this to come out wrong, but he has a great rear end."

WHALERS COACH PAUL HOLMGREN, ON ANDREI NIKOLISHIN

"I have to go through a couple pairs of shorts each game, but other than that, it's great."

COYOTES COACH BOB FRANCIS, ON THE TIGHT 2001-02 PLAYOFF RACE

"Looks frightening from the bench. He's going to scare his kids with that thing."

DALLAS STARS COACH KEN HITCHCOCK, ON DALLAS STAR ROMAN TUREK'S NEW MASK

"I don't like my hockey sticks touching other sticks, and I don't like them crossing one another, and I kind of have them hidden in the corner. I put baby powder on the ends. I think it's essentially a matter of taking care of what takes care of you."

OILER WAYNE GRETZKY

"If you jumped out of a plane without a parachute, would that prove that you were brave?"

HALL OF FAME GOALIE JACQUES PLANTE, ASKED IF WEARING A MASK PROVED THAT HE WAS AFRAID

"We've got no-trade clauses. Nobody wants us."

FLYER KEITH JONES, DESCRIBING HIMSELF AND CRAIG BERUBE

"Really, there are none. We traded him for a 10th round pick in a nine-round draft."

FLYERS GM BOBBY CLARKE, ON WHAT "FUTURE CONSIDERATIONS" HE RECEIVED FROM THE NASHVILLE PREDATORS FOR SERGEI KLIMENTIEV

"It's tough for a player to talk about trades, because when a player talks about a trade that's like throwing a teammate under the bus."

FLYER JEREMY ROENICK, ON HIS MIXED FEELINGS WHEN A GOOD PLAYER IS RUMORED TO BE COMING TO HIS CLUB

The first thing I would do when I saw Bobby coming down at me was to say a little prayer if I had time. I'm sure I wasn't the only goalie who did that.

HALL OF FAME MAPLE LEAF   , ABOUT BOBBY HULL

"If you're winning, you'll be rewarded and if you're losing, changes will be made. It happened when I played and it'll happen 100 years from now."

COYOTES MANAGING PARTNER **WAYNE GRETZKY**, ON TRADES

"I don't care if we lose every game for the next five years and the team goes broke and moves to Moose Jaw. I will not trade Pavel Bure!"

CANUCKS GM **BRIAN BURKE**, SEVERAL WEEKS BEFORE TRADING BURE TO THE PANTHERS

"The kid looks good in his first game."

WHALER **GORDIE HOWE**, AT AGE 51, AFTER 41-YEAR-OLD BOBBY HULL
MADE HIS 1979 HARTFORD WHALER DEBUT

"The average guy gets sophisticated when they get older and they get cynical and they think there's better things to do with their life. But not [Gordie] Howe or [Rocket] Richard. They understood that hockey was the greatest thing they'd ever do."

FLAMES ASSISTANT GM AND FORMER PLAYER **AL MACNEIL**

"He's skating like he's 36 again."

DALLAS STAR MIKE KEANE, AFTER 38-YEAR-OLD TEAMMATE GUY CARBONNEAU
HAD A GREAT GAME

"He's as old as some trees."

MAPLE LEAF COACH PAT BURNS, ON VETERAN MAPLE LEAF MIKE GARTNER

"I played my age. Not bad."

HURRICANE RON FRANCIS, AFTER PLAYING 39 MINUTES IN THE THIRD GAME OF THE 2002
STANLEY CUP FINAL

"Luc Robitaille is a great kid and a good player, but ask
anybody on the street and they'd probably think Luc
Robitaille is a type of salad dressing."

L.A. KINGS OWNER BRUCE MCNALL, ON WHY HE HAD TO BRING WAYNE GRETZKY
TO LOS ANGELES IN 1988

"I was never going to be a player to get standing ovations
in a visitor's building. I realized from Day One, the way I
played, I'd never be a Gretzky or a Lemieux. Well, a Mario,
I mean."

AVALANCHE CLAUDE LEMIEUX, ON GETTING USED TO BEING HATED
BY OPPOSING PLAYERS AND FANS

"When no one else signs me."

RED WING CHRIS CHELIOS, ON WHEN IT WILL BE TIME TO RETIRE

"You miss 100 percent of the shots you never take."

OILER WAYNE GRETZKY

"**Not only is there more to life** than basketball, there's a lot **more** to **basketball** than **basketball**."

LONGTIME CHICAGO BULLS AND LOS ANGELES LAKERS COACH PHIL JACKSON

"There are really only two plays: Romeo and Juliet and put
the darn ball in the basket."

LONGTIME NCAA COACH ABE LEMONS

"The only difference between a good shot and a bad shot is
if it goes in or not."

NBA STAR TURNED BROADCASTER CHARLES BARKLEY

"Finish last in your league and they call you idiot. Finish last
in medical school and they call you doctor."

FAMED NCAA COACH ABE LEMONS

"I keep both eyes on my man. The basket hasn't moved on
me yet."

BASKETBALL SUPERSTAR JULIUS ERVING

"Sometimes that light at the end of the tunnel is a train."

NBA LEGEND AND BROADCASTER CHARLES BARKLEY

"They say that nobody is perfect.
Then they tell you practice makes perfect.
I wish they'd make up their minds."

NBA LEGEND WILT CHAMBERLAIN

"If you can figure it out, I'm going to tell you to resign, and I will double your salary to sit on the bench."

TORONTO RAPTORS COACH SAM MITCHELL, WHEN ASKED WHAT IT WOULD TAKE
TO MAKE THE INCONSISTENT JOEY GRAHAM CONSISTENTLY GOOD

"They called us the Cinderella team, and we played like we were going to turn into a pumpkin."

OHIO STATE COACH FRED TAYLOR EXPLAINS AN 80-66 LOSS
TO NORTH CAROLINA IN THE NCAA TOURNAMENT

"This year we plan to run and shoot. Next season we hope to run and score."

UNIVERSITY OF OKLAHOMA COACH BILLY TUBBS

"He has the shooting range. What he doesn't have is the making range."

PRINCETON COACH PETE CARRIL ON WHY HE WOULDN'T MOVE STEVE GOODRICH
FROM CENTER TO FORWARD

"I'm trying to do too much and I'm thinking too much and I'm thinking about trying to do too much."

UNIVERSITY OF KANSAS GUARD TONY GUY TRIES TO EXPLAIN HIS SHOOTING SLUMP

"If a guy pays you five dollars, you give him **seven dollars worth of work.**"

BOSTON CELTICS LEGEND BILL RUSSELL

"We can alley, but we don't have the oop."

OKLAHOMA CITY UNIVERSITY COACH ABE LEMONS EXPLAINS WHY HIS TEAM
MESSED UP AN ALLEY-OOP ATTEMPT

"Don't put me back in."

UNIVERSITY OF MEMPHIS GUARD ANTONIO ANDERSON TO COACH JOHN CALIPARI WHILE
WATCHING BACKUP DONEAL MACK MAKE SEVEN THREE-POINTERS IN THE SECOND HALF

"Coming off the bench is tough. As soon as you don't produce, the starters are coming back."

TORONTO RAPTOR KRIS HUMPHRIES

"I don't want some turkey to look good and then have to play him the next five games."

UNIVERSITY OF TEXAS COACH ABE LEMONS EXPLAINING WHY HE DIDN'T LIKE
TO MAKE PLAYER SUBSTITUTIONS WHEN HIS TEAM WAS LOSING

"He changes your shots when he's in the game. He also changes your shots when he's out of the game because you get so used to trying to throw it over him, you forget when he's not there."

11-YEAR NBA VETERAN CLIFF LEVINGSTON ON PLAYING AGAINST 7-FOOT-4 UTAH JAZZ CENTER
MARK EATON

"My mother had to send me to the movies with my birth certificate so that I wouldn't have to pay the extra 50 cents that the adults had to pay."

NBA SUPERSTAR KAREEM ABDUL-JABBAR

"When everybody else is tired, he's still going to be tall."

"Quick guys get tired. Big guys don't shrink."

"Everybody pulls for David, nobody roots for Goliath."

"Red used to never have a curfew. I asked him why he never had a curfew. He said, 'Because I have to be there to enforce it.'"

"My training rule is 'don't get caught.'"

"When a coach is hired, he's fired. The date just hasn't been filled in yet."

"I'll always remember Tom Heinsohn's pep talks. One time there were 72 bleeps in it — and that was Christmas Day."

"They measured me when I was sitting down."

SUDANESE-BORN 7-FOOT-7 NBA STAR **MANUTE BOL** ON WHY HIS PASSPORT LISTED HIM AS 5-FOOT-2

"He doesn't shine them. He sends them through a car wash."

UCLA STAR **LYNN SHACKELFORD** ON BOB LANIER'S SIZE 22 SHOES

"I am 7 feet 4 with my shoes on, and I always play with my shoes on."

WHY U.S. OLYMPIC BASKETBALL TEAM CENTER **TOM BURLESON** WASN'T BOTHERED BY REPORTS THAT HE WAS ONLY 7 FEET 2 WHEN MEASURED BAREFOOT

"Charles joined my family for a day at the beach last summer, and my children asked if they could go in the ocean. I had to tell them, 'Not right now, kids. Charles is using it.'"

PHILADELPHIA 76ERS GENERAL MANAGER **PAT WILLIAMS** ON 260-POUND ROOKIE CHARLES BARKLEY

"No, ma'am. I'm a jockey for a dinosaur."

6-FOOT-9 CHICAGO BULLS CENTER **JOHNNY KERR**, WHEN ASKED IF HE WAS A BASKETBALL PLAYER

"No, I clean giraffe ears."

6-FOOT-10 WASHINGTON BULLETS STAR **ELVIN HAYES**, WHEN ASKED IF HE WAS A BASKETBALL PLAYER

"I got bald."

PHILADELPHIA 76ERS COACH **ALEX HANNUM**, WHEN ASKED WHY HE WAS LISTED AT 6 FOOT 8 AS A PLAYER BUT ONLY 6 FOOT 7 AS A COACH

"We have black players, white players, a Mormon and four Yugoslavians. Our toughest decision isn't what offense or defense to run but what type of warm-up music to play."

WAGNER COLLEGE COACH TIM CAPSTRAW

"All right, who's playing for second?"

BOSTON CELTICS LEGEND LARRY BIRD BEFORE A THREE-POINT SHOOTING CONTEST

"What excites me the most is when a coach calls a time-out and chews out his forward because I just dunked on his head."

UTAH JAZZ SUPERSTAR KARL MALONE

"When you go out there and do the things you're supposed to do, people view you as selfish."

NBA LEGEND WILT CHAMBERLAIN

"There is no 'I' in team but there is in win."

CHICAGO BULLS SUPERSTAR MICHAEL JORDAN

"We would set up a zone defense that had four men around the key, and I guarded the basket. When the other team took a shot, I'd just go up and tap it out."

BASKETBALL LEGEND GEORGE MIKAN, THE GAME'S FIRST "BIG MAN" AT 6 FOOT 10, AND THE REASON GOALTENDING WAS MADE ILLEGAL

"If you don't have time to do it right, when will you have time to do it over?"

LONGTIME UCLA COACH JOHN WOODEN

"My biggest thrill came the night Elgin Baylor and I combined for 73 points in Madison Square Garden. Elgin had 71 of them."

FORMER LOS ANGELES LAKER "HOT" ROD HUNDLEY

"Going into the series I thought Michael had 2,000 moves. I was wrong. He has 3,000."

PHOENIX TRAIL BLAZERS STAR CLYDE DREXLER ON MICHAEL JORDAN,
AFTER JORDAN'S CHICAGO BULLS BEAT THE BLAZERS FOR THE 1992 NBA CHAMPIONSHIP

"We're shooting 100 percent — 60 percent from the field and 40 percent from the free-throw line."

UNIVERSITY OF MISSOURI COACH NORM STEWART

"Chemistry is a class you take in high school or college where you figure out two plus two is 10 or something."

NBA STAR DENNIS RODMAN

"We all get heavier as we get older because there's a lot more information in our heads. Our heads weigh more."

LOS ANGELES LAKERS CENTER VLADE DIVAC EXPLAINS WHY HE REPORTED
TO TRAINING CAMP 15 POUNDS HEAVIER

"These young guys are playing checkers. I'm out there playing chess."

LOS ANGELES LAKERS STAR KOBE BRYANT

"I want my teams to have my personality — surly, obnoxious and arrogant."

MARQUETTE COACH **AL MCGUIRE**

"A man has to know his limitations, and I don't have any."

NBA JOURNEYMAN **EDGAR JONES**

"Basketball is like war, in that offensive weapons are developed first, and it always takes a while for the defense to catch up."

LEGENDARY BOSTON CELTICS COACH **RED AUERBACH**

"There's no such thing as coulda, shoulda and woulda. If you shoulda and coulda, you woulda done it."

LOS ANGELES LAKERS COACH PAT RILEY

"A lot of bad things happened to us. First, Auburn played well."

LONGTIME VANDERBILT COACH C.M. NEWTON EXPLAINS A LOSS TO AUBURN

"I was hoping Vanderbilt wouldn't bring their 'A' game and that we'd have a shot."

UNIVERSITY OF MASSACHUSETTS COACH TRAVIS FORD AFTER VANDERBILT SCORED
61 POINTS IN THE SECOND HALF FOR A 97-88 VICTORY

"I think this whole game hinged on one call — the one I made last April scheduling this game."

UNIVERSITY OF MAINE COACH PETER GAVETT ON A SEASON-OPENING 115-57 LOSS
TO 7-FOOT-4 CENTER RALPH SAMPSON AND THE UNIVERSITY OF VIRGINIA CAVALIERS

"It's hard to be fit as a fiddle when you're shaped like a cello."

UTAH JAZZ COACH FRANK LAYDEN EXPLAINS WHY HE WAS TRYING
TO GET A 300-POUND PLAYER TO SLIM DOWN

"The worst thing our players did was fail to grow taller."

DUKE UNIVERSITY WOMEN'S BASKETBALL COACH DEBBIE LEONARD AFTER A 103-39 LOSS

"I designed the play without realizing what big feet Larry has. I should have moved him over 6 inches in my diagram."

KANSAS CITY KINGS COACH **PHIL JOHNSON** AFTER GUARD LARRY DREW STEPPED ON THE OUT-OF-BOUNDS LINE, NULLIFYING A LAST-SECOND SHOT THAT WOULD HAVE BEATEN THE HOUSTON ROCKETS

"I bought a Stairmaster. I stare at it every day."

NBA STAR AND TV COMMENTATOR **CHARLES BARKLEY** ON EXERCISE

"You can't play if you're dead."

PHILADELPHIA 76ERS STAR **CHARLES BARKLEY** ON WHY HE FINISHED LAST IN THE TEAM'S 2-MILE TRAINING CAMP RUN

"Failure is good. It's fertilizer. Everything I've learned about coaching, I've learned from making mistakes."

LONGTIME NCAA AND NBA COACH **RICK PITINO**

"I can accept failure, but I can't accept not trying."

CHICAGO BULLS LEGEND **MICHAEL JORDAN**

"I liked the choreography, but I didn't care for the costumes."

TOMMY TUNE, 6-FOOT-6 1/2 BROADWAY SINGER-DANCER-ACTOR-DIRECTOR, EXPLAINS WHY HE NEVER CONSIDERED PLAYING BASKETBALL

"Yao Ming is basically what they call him, the **Great Wall** of **China.** Once he gets the ball, he's pretty much **unstoppable."**

CHARLOTTE BOBCATS FORWARD GERALD WALLACE
ON THE HOUSTON ROCKETS' CHINESE SUPERSTAR

"Hearing the crowd was great. It made what little hair I have stand on end."

DENVER NUGGETS STAR ALEX ENGLISH RECALLS THE STANDING OVATION HE RECEIVED
AFTER SCORING 54 POINTS AGAINST THE HOUSTON ROCKETS

"I threw a left hook, but I was backpedaling so fast it never got there."

FORMER BALTIMORE BULLET CENTER BOB FERRY GIVES HIS VERSION OF A FIGHT
WITH WILT CHAMBERLAIN OF THE PHILADELPHIA 76ERS

"I knew I was dog meat. Luckily, I'm the high-priced dog meat that everybody wants. I'm the good-quality dog meat. I'm the Alpo of the NBA."

NBA SUPERSTAR SHAQUILLE O'NEAL

"He's about as safe as me in a room full of cookies. If I'm in a room full of cookies, the cookies ain't got no damn chance."

NBA STAR AND BROADCASTER CHARLES BARKLEY ON NEW YORK KNICKS COACH
ISIAH THOMAS'S JOB SECURITY AFTER A 45-POINT LOSS TO THE BOSTON CELTICS

"Don't get caught looking at the apple in case someone takes the ladder away."

TORONTO RAPTORS COACH LENNY WILKINS ON THE POSSIBILITY OF WINNING A DIVISION TITLE

"I thought he was going to hit me first, so I hit him first."

WHY SEATTLE SUPERSONICS FORWARD XAVIER MCDANIEL GOT INTO A FIGHT
WITH KEVIN WILLIS OF THE ATLANTA HAWKS

"When you're playing him, it's like going through the Tunnel of Love. All you feel is hands, knees and elbows all over you."

NEW YORK KNICKS STAR WALT FRAZIER ON WHY CHICAGO'S JERRY SLOAN
WAS SO TOUGH DEFENSIVELY

"Saltwater taffy."

PORTLAND TRAIL BLAZERS CENTER CALDWELL JONES,
WHEN ASKED TO NAME HIS FAVORITE SEAFOOD

"You put the toast in the toaster, and it ain't done until the toaster says, 'Ding.'"

NBA SUPERSTAR SHAQUILLE O'NEAL PONDERS WHEN HE'D BE READY
TO RETURN FROM AN INJURY

"Too much coffee. Too much coffee and Gatorade. It's a hell of a mix. If you're ever tired in the morning, just try that mix and tell me what you think."

MINNESOTA TIMBERWOLVES STAR KEVIN GARNETT

"We have 44 defenses to stop him, but he has 45 ways to score."

GOLDEN STATE WARRIORS COACH AL ATTLES ON NATE "TINY" ARCHIBALD

"I've got a theory that if you give 100 percent all of the time, somehow things will work out in the end."

BOSTON CELTICS HALL OF FAMER LARRY BIRD

"I always keep a ball in the car. You never know."

HOUSTON ROCKETS STAR HAKEEM OLAJUWON

"After I played him for the first time, I said 'Let's see. He's four or five inches taller. He's 40 or 50 pounds heavier. His vertical leap is at least as good as mine. He can get up and down the floor as well as I can. And he's smart. The real problem with all this is I have to show up.'"

BOSTON CELTICS GREAT BILL RUSSELL
ON FIRST FACING FELLOW NBA LEGEND WILT CHAMBERLAIN

"I used to think that Michael Jordan was the Babe Ruth of basketball. I have now come to believe that Babe Ruth was the Michael Jordan of baseball."

CHICAGO BULLS OWNER JERRY REINSDORF

"We cut him off and there was nowhere for him to go but out of bounds ... It's still the greatest move I've ever seen in basketball, the all-time greatest."

LOS ANGELES LAKERS SUPERSTAR MAGIC JOHNSON RECALLS JULIUS ERVING'S LAYUP
FROM BEHIND THE BASKET IN THE 1980 NBA FINALS

"We all thought he was a movie-star player, but we found out he wears a hard hat. It's like finding a great orthopedic surgeon who can also operate a bulldozer."

LOS ANGELES LAKERS COACH PAUL WESTHEAD AFTER ROOKIE GUARD MAGIC JOHNSON FILLED IN AT CENTER FOR THE INJURED KAREEM ABDUL-JABBAR AND SCORED 42 POINTS WITH 15 REBOUNDS IN A 123-107 WIN OVER THE PHILADELPHIA 76ERS IN GAME SIX TO WIN THE 1980 NBA CHAMPIONSHIP

"If I'm going to play against Abdul-Jabbar, I'd like to have a month's notice. "

BOSTON CELTIC JIM ARD

"They don't pay you a million dollars for two-hand chest passes."

HALL OF FAMER PETE MARAVICH

"When I dunk, I put something on it. I want the ball to hit the floor before I do."

BACKBOARDING-BREAKING DUNK-SUPERSTAR DARRYL DAWKINS

"I'm not a role model. Just because I dunk a basketball doesn't mean I should raise your kids. "

NBA STAR CHARLES BARKLEY

"GO FOR THE MOON. IF YOU DON'T GET IT, YOU'LL STILL BE HEADING FOR A STAR."

NEW YORK KNICKS HALL OF FAMER WILLIS REED

"Rice defends against the free throw as well as anybody I've ever seen."

TEXAS A&M BASKETBALL COACH **SHELBY METCALFE** AFTER WATCHING BAYLOR UNIVERSITY MISS 19 OF 35 FREE THROWS AGAINST RICE

"Half of them were bad calls."

NBA LEGEND **KAREEM ABDUL-JABBAR** AFTER ESTABLISHING A CAREER RECORD WITH 4,194 FOULS

"It is unbelievably frustrating to remain in a rugged occupation with waning skills."

BOSTON CELTICS STAR **DAVE COWENS** ON HIS DECISION TO RETIRE

"I knew it was time to retire when I was driving down the lane and got called for a three-second violation."

FORMER NBA PLAYER AND COACH **JOHNNY KERR**

"I'm 36. I could have waved the towel too aggressively for all I know."

DALLAS MAVERICK **SCOTT WILLIAMS**, WHO WASN'T SURE HOW HE'D SUFFERED A SLIGHT STOMACH STRAIN

"Everybody looks at how many years you play. They forget about what you do to slow down Father Time. You can't beat him, but you can sure slow him down."

36-YEAR-OLD UTAH JAZZ STAR **KARL MALONE**, WHO PLAYED UNTIL HE WAS 40

"I don't have the physical talent those guys have. My hard work has made me very good."

INDIANA PACERS STAR **REGGIE MILLER** ON WHY HE DIDN'T RATE HIMSELF
AMONG MICHAEL JORDAN, SCOTTIE PIPPEN, GRANT HILL AND SHAQUILLE O'NEAL
AS THE BEST PLAYERS IN THE NBA

"I don't know if I practiced more than anybody, but I sure practiced enough. I still wonder if somebody — somewhere — was practicing more than me."

BOSTON CELTICS SUPERSTAR **LARRY BIRD**

"Excellence is the gradual result of always striving to do better."

MIAMI HEAT COACH **PAT RILEY**

"Good, better, best. Never let it rest. Until your good is better and your better is best."

SAN ANTONIO SPURS STAR **TIM DUNCAN**

"Nothing will work unless you do."

LEGENDARY UCLA COACH **JOHN WOODEN**

"It doesn't bother me. I was also my wife's second choice, and we've been married for 25 years."

UNIVERSITY OF OKLAHOMA COACH **BILLY TUBBS** EXPLAINS WHY IT DIDN'T BOTHER HIM
THAT HE WAS THE TEAM'S SECOND CHOICE

"We're experts at bouncin', not pronouncin'."

GEESE AUSBIE OF THE HARLEM GLOBETROTTERS HAS DIFFICULTIES
WITH THE NAME OF CHINESE DEPUTY PREMIER TENG HSIAO-PING

"Then you'd know what I was saying to you."

UNIVERSITY OF INDIANA CENTER **UWE BLAB** EXPLAINING TO COACH BOBBY KNIGHT
WHY HE WOULDN'T GIVE HIM ANY GERMAN SWEAR WORDS TO USE ON THE REFEREES

"Be a dreamer. If you don't know how to dream, you're dead."

NORTH CAROLINA STATE COACH **JIM VALVANO**

"When you lose a 'must' game, it wasn't a 'must' game."

NEW YORK KNICKS TRAINER **DANNY WHELAN**

"You can't let praise or criticism get to you. It's a weakness to get caught up in either one."

UCLA COACH **JOHN WOODEN**

"There are only two options regarding commitment. You're either in or you're out. There's no such thing as life in between."

MIAMI HEAT COACH **PAT RILEY**

I don't care what people think. People are stupid.

NBA STAR TURNED COMMENTATOR

CHARLES BARKLEY

"It's one thing to hear about it from your coach, but when your wife tells you it stinks, you tend to work on it."

13-YEAR NBA VETERAN **ORLANDO WOOLRIDGE** ON A DEFICIENCY IN HIS GAME

"Uh, yeah. I mean, it's tough to say, woulda, shoulda, coulda, ifs and buts like candy and nuts, you know, you never know. This, that and the other thing. Who knows? You know, there's a lot of what-ifs. You know, my whole life is a lot of what-ifs."

TORONTO RAPTOR **MATT BONNER** WHEN ASKED IF THE TEAM RESENTED FORMER RAPTOR VINCE CARTER

"I can't really remember the names of the clubs that we went to."

LOS ANGELES LAKERS STAR **SHAQUILLE O'NEAL** IN ANSWER TO A QUESTION ABOUT WHETHER OR NOT HE VISITED THE PARTHENON WHILE IN GREECE

"That was my fault. I should have read it before it came out."

PHILADELPHIA 76ERS STAR **CHARLES BARKLEY** ON BEING MISQUOTED IN HIS AUTOBIOGRAPHY

"Shaq is not the man. He's the man because the NBA wants him to be the man, but before you can be the man, you've got to be the man."

NBA VETERAN **DENNIS RODMAN** DISCUSSES THE YOUNG SHAQUILLE O'NEAL

"I've learned that there's a time when it's in the team's interest not to say anything, and in some instances not saying anything is really saying a lot. A lot of people understand what not saying anything means, so, in effect, not saying anything is really saying a lot."

OUTSPOKEN PORTLAND TRAIL BLAZERS STAR **BILL WALTON**

"It's almost as if we have ESPN."

LOS ANGELES LAKERS SUPERSTAR **MAGIC JOHNSON** ON PLAYING WITH JAMES WORTHY

"I am an equal-opportunity hater."

TORONTO RAPTORS COACH **SAM MITCHELL**

"I don't have the first clue who he is talking about because all I worry about is Jerome."

SEATTLE SUPERSONICS CENTER **JEROME JAMES** AFTER COACH NATE MCMILLAN
CHARGED THAT HE WAS SELFISH

"Left hand, right hand, it doesn't matter. I'm amphibious."

NBA JOURNEYMAN **CHARLES SHACKLEFORD**

"If it ain't broke, don't break it."

19-YEAR NBA VETERAN **CHARLES OAKLEY**

231

"It's not how good you can play when you play good. It's how good you play when you play bad, and we can play bad as good as anyone in the country."

UNIVERSITY OF GEORGIA COACH HUGH DURHAM

"Up and down."

HOUSTON ROCKETS GUARD VERNON MAXWELL, WHEN ASKED BY COACH DON CHANEY
TO GIVE A ONE-WORD DESCRIPTION OF HIS SEASON

"He has to wear low-cuts. The high-tops go over his knees."

A BOSTON CELTICS TV ANNOUNCER ON THE FOOTWEAR CHOICE OF 5-FOOT-3
MUGGSY BOGUES OF THE CHARLOTTE HORNETS

"Any time Detroit scores more than a hundred points and holds the other team below a hundred points they almost always win."

DETROIT PISTONS COACH DOUG COLLINS

"It's not going to be peaches and gravy all the time."

INDIANA PACERS CENTER BRAD MILLER ON HIS TEAM'S STRUGGLES

"I sight down my nose to shoot, and now my nose isn't straight since I broke it."

CENTENARY COLLEGE PLAYER BARRIE HAYNIE EXPLAINS HIS SHOOTING WOES

"I threw my arms up and one just kept going."

"You scored one more point than a dead man."

"We have a great bunch of outside shooters. Unfortunately, all our games are played indoors."

"What do you have when you have an agent buried up to his neck in sand? Not enough sand."

"You could tell five guys to go over to the post office at 2 o'clock and one of 'em wouldn't be there, so why have so many trick plays?"

"My sister's expecting a baby, and I don't know if I'm going to be an uncle or an aunt."

"The main thing to remember about **Michael is that God only made one.**"

CHICAGO BULLS ASSISTANT COACH **JOHN BACH** ON MICHAEL JORDAN

"You can practice shooting eight hours a day, but if your technique is wrong, then all you become is very good at shooting the wrong way. Get the fundamentals down, and the level of everything you do will rise."

CHICAGO BULLS SUPERSTAR MICHAEL JORDAN

"I'm expecting. Well, I'm not. That would be weird."

CLEVELAND CAVALIERS STAR LEBRON JAMES, WHOSE GIRLFRIEND WAS DUE TO DELIVER HIS SECOND SON

"There were enough bad passes and missed free throws to knock out any theories about coaching being responsible."

BOSTON CELTICS COACH BILL FITCH AFTER A GAME SEVEN PLAYOFF LOSS TO THE PHILADELPHIA 76ERS

"When it comes to stitches and bruises, I've definitely been in the Christmas spirit in my career. I give more than I receive."

DALLAS MAVERICKS CENTER SHAWN BRADLEY

"When we were playing the Celtics once around Christmastime, Larry Bird pulled up for a three right in front of our bench and said, 'Merry Christmas.'"

TRASH-TALKING INDIANA PACERS STAR REGGIE MILLER ON THE BEST THING HE'D HEARD SOMEONE ELSE SAY ON THE COURT

"I'm tired of hearing about money, money, money, money, money. I just want to play the game, drink Pepsi, wear Reebok."

LOS ANGELES LAKERS STAR SHAQUILLE O'NEAL

"If I weren't earning $3 million a year to dunk a basketball, most people on the street would run in the other direction if they saw me coming."

PHILADELPHIA 76ERS STAR CHARLES BARKLEY

"Everything's great until we start playing, and you guys start telling me I'm not worth the money."

TORONTO RAPTORS COACH SAM MITCHELL TO THE MEDIA IN THE OFF-SEASON
SHORTLY AFTER SIGNING A NEW FOUR-YEAR $16-MILLION CONTRACT

"I really don't like talking about money. All I can say is that the Good Lord must have wanted me to have it."

BOSTON CELTICS SUPERSTAR LARRY BIRD

"I didn't miss the smell of the gym, the bounce of the ball or the kids. I just ran out of money."

MISSISSIPPI STATE UNIVERSITY COACH BOB BOYD EXPLAINS HIS DECISION
TO RETURN AFTER A TWO-YEAR RETIREMENT

"Omelets for dinner? This is the best day of my life!"

CLEVELAND CAVALIERS STAR LEBRON JAMES,
GUEST VOICING ON THE SIMPSONS

"That was a good day too."

LEBRON AGAIN, AFTER LISA SIMPSON REMINDED HIM
HE HAD JUST SIGNED A $90-MILLION CONTRACT

"We might make a lot of money, but we also spend a lot of money."

NEW YORK KNICKS STAR PATRICK EWING

"Sport is the only profession I know of that, when you retire, you have to go to work."

NBA HALL OF FAMER EARL "THE PEARL" MONROE

"I can't imagine working nine-to-five. I think that would suck."

NBA STAR TURNED BROADCASTER CHARLES BARKLEY

"If you make every game a life and death proposition, you're going to have problems. For one thing, you'll be dead a lot."

UNIVERSITY OF NORTH CAROLINA COACHING LEGEND DEAN SMITH

"The strong take from the weak, and the smart take from the strong."

PRINCETON BASKETBALL COACH PETE CARRIL

"They said playing basketball would kill me. Well, not playing basketball was killing me."

LOS ANGELES LAKERS STAR MAGIC JOHNSON ON HIS COMEBACK FROM RETIREMENT AFTER BEING DIAGNOSED HIV POSITIVE

"That and a dollar leaves you with a dollar."

MAVERICKS OWNER **MARK CUBAN** ON DALLAS BEING THE BEST TEAM DURING THE 2006-07
REGULAR SEASON. (THE MAVS WERE UPSET IN THE FIRST ROUND OF THE PLAYOFFS)

"People say I enjoy being famous. I don't. But what choice do I have?"

NBA LEGEND AND TV COMMENTATOR **CHARLES BARKLEY**

"The secret is to have eight great players, and four others who will cheer like crazy."

UNLV COACH **JERRY TARKANIAN** ON WINNING

"The main ingredient of stardom is the rest of the team."

CELEBRATED UCLA COACH **JOHN WOODEN**

"You can say something to popes, kings and presidents, but you can't talk to officials. In the next war, they ought to give everybody a whistle."

UNIVERSITY OF TEXAS COACH **ABE LEMONS**

"I wanted to have a career in sports when I was young, but I had to give it up. I'm only 6 feet tall, so I couldn't play basketball. I'm only 190 pounds, so I couldn't play football. And I have 20-20 vision, so I couldn't be a referee."

TONIGHT SHOW HOST **JAY LENO**

241

"**WE'RE GOING TO TURN THIS TEAM AROUND 360 DEGREES.**"

NEW YORK NETS STAR **JASON KIDD**

"Officiating is the only occupation in the world where the highest accolade is silence."

NBA REFEREE EARL STROM

"Pressure can burst a pipe, or pressure can make a diamond."

NBA VETERAN ROBERT HORRY

"I told the NBA people I was only available on days ending in Y."

EASTERN LEAGUE REFEREE ROGER MCCANN AFTER BEING PRESSED
INTO EMERGENCY SERVICE FOR AN NBA GAME

"I don't count 'em, I just call 'em."

NBA REFEREE EARL STROM ANSWERING COMPLAINTS THAT HE WAS CALLING TOO MANY FOULS
AGAINST THE COMPLAINING TEAM

"I'm not going to say anything about the officiating because it might take two days."

IOWA STATE COACH JOHNNY ORR AFTER HIS TEAM GOT ONLY NINE FREE THROW ATTEMPTS
TO HIS OPPONENTS' 35 IN A 73-70 LOSS TO MISSOURI

"The trouble with the officials is they just don't care who wins."

CENTENARY COLLEGE COACH TOMMY CANTERBURY

"Larry Bird just throws the ball in the air, and God moves the basket underneath it."

CLEVELAND CAVALIERS PUBLIC ADDRESS ANNOUNCER HOWIE CHIZEK AFTER THE BOSTON STAR SET A CLUB RECORD WITH 60 POINTS IN ONE GAME AND SCORED 48 IN ANOTHER AGAINST THE CAVS DURING THE 1984-85 SEASON

"He is the most exciting, awesome player in the game today. I think it's just God disguised as Michael Jordan."

BOSTON CELTICS SUPERSTAR LARRY BIRD AFTER MICHAEL JORDAN SCORED 63 POINTS AGAINST THE CELTICS IN A 1986 PLAYOFF GAME

"If you meet the Buddha in the lane, feed him the ball."

LONGTIME CHICAGO BULLS AND LOS ANGELES LAKERS COACH PHIL JACKSON

"I know this kid was good, but he's gooder than I thought."

SHAQ ON DWYANE WADE

"When it comes to ridiculization, if you can't walk in a man's shoes, you shouldn't ridicule him."

SHAQUILLE O'NEAL

"I'm a very quotatious person."

SHAQUILLE O'NEAL

"Baryshnikov was great, but the play needs a shot clock."

BASKETBALL COMMENTATOR **BUCKY WATERS** AFTER WATCHING MIKHAIL BARYSHNIKOV IN A
SHOW BASED ON FRANZ KAFKA'S METAMORPHOSIS

"The difference between those three is in The Godfather
trilogy. One is Fredo, who was never ready for me to hand it
over to him. One is Sonny, who will do whatever it takes to
be the man. And one is Michael, who if you watch the
trilogy, the Godfather hands it over to Michael. So I have no
problem handing it over to Dwyane."

NBA SUPERSTAR **SHAQUILLE O'NEAL** ON HIS RELATIONSHIPS WITH PENNY HARDAWAY,
KOBE BRYANT AND DWYANE WADE

"In my prime I could have handled Michael Jordan.
Of course, he would be only 12 years old."

NBA PLAYER TURNED COACH **JERRY SLOAN**

"Winning is overrated. The only time it is really important
is in surgery and war."

TV ANALYST AND FORMER MARQUETTE UNIVERSITY COACH **AL MCGUIRE**

"He's not that good. It's all computer-generated."

CLEVELAND CAVALIER **SCOTT POLLARD** ON TEAMMATE LEBRON JAMES

"Tom."

"I thank my teammates for letting their men blow by them."

MIAMI HEAT CENTER ALONZO MOURNING, JOKING AFTER WINNING HIS SECOND STRAIGHT
DEFENSIVE PLAYER OF THE YEAR AWARD IN 2000

"I've been here so long that when I got here, the Dead Sea wasn't even sick."

UNIVERSITY OF ALABAMA COACH WIMP SANDERSON ON LASTING 32 YEARS AT THE SCHOOL

"Now that I'm in Detroit I'd like to change my name to Abdul Automobile."

DETROIT PISTONS FORWARD M.L. CARR

"Don't you ever pass?"

NBA LEGEND BOB COUSY AFTER TEAMMATE BILL SHARMAN'S LENGTH-OF-THE-COURT ATTEMPTED
PASS TO HIM SWISHED THROUGH THE NET FOR A BASKET DURING THE 1957 NBA ALL-STAR GAME

"I'd rather be a football coach. That way you can lose only 11 games a season. I lost 11 games in December alone."

PAN AMERICAN COLLEGE COACH ABE LEMONS

"Too bad he wasn't 40."

SPRINGFIELD COLLEGE COACH ED BILIK AFTER FORWARD IVAN OLIVARES
SCORED 24 POINTS ON HIS 24TH BIRTHDAY

"One day of practice is like one day of clean living. It doesn't do you any good."

LONGTIME NCAA BASKETBALL COACH
ABE LEMONS

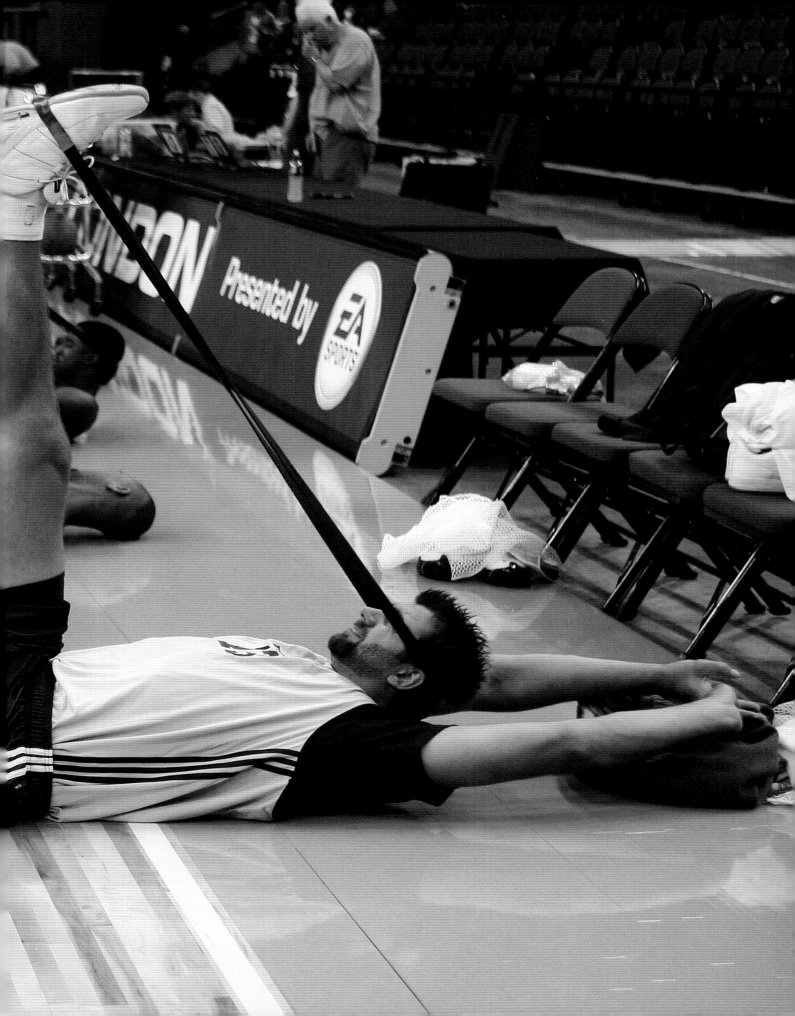

"Kids are great. That's one of the best things about our business, all the kids you get to meet. It's a shame they have to grow up to be regular people and come to the games and call you names."

NBA STAR CHARLES BARKLEY

"We had a lot of nicknames — Scarface, Blackie, Toothless — and those were just the cheerleaders."

UTAH JAZZ COACH FRANK LAYDEN REMEMBERS HIS HIGH SCHOOL DAYS IN BROOKLYN

"If I could look into the future, I wouldn't be sitting here talking to you doorknobs. I'd be out investing in the stock market."

BOSTON CELTICS GREAT KEVIN MCHALE, WHEN ASKED TO ASSESS HIS TEAM'S PROSPECTS IN AN UPCOMING SEASON

"I don't think we would have won that game if we didn't have the plane."

SACRAMENTO KINGS COACH DICK MOTTA JUSTIFIES THE EXPENSE OF A PRIVATE PLANE AFTER THE TEAM WENT 1-40 ON THE ROAD

"If we stay free of injuries, we'll be in contention to be a healthy team."

NEW JERSEY NET CHRIS MORRIS, WHEN ASKED ABOUT HIS TEAM'S CHANCES IN 1993

"He looks like he went to the blood bank and forgot to say when."

PHILADELPHIA 76ERS GENERAL MANAGER **PAT WILLIAMS**, WHEN ASKED ABOUT THE 7-FOOT-7 BUT RAIL-THIN MANUTE BOL

"I've never heard of a plane that backed into a mountain."

VANDERBILT COACH **C.M. NEWTON** EXPLAINS HIS HABIT OF SITTING IN THE LAST SEAT ON TEAM FLIGHTS

"I hate it. It looks like a stickup at a 7-Eleven. Five guys standing there with their hands in the air."

LONGTIME NCAA COACH **NORM SLOAN** DESCRIBES ZONE DEFENSE

"Ask not what your teammates can do for you. Ask what you can do for your teammates."

LOS ANGELES LAKERS STAR **MAGIC JOHNSON**

"I'd much rather be second fiddle on a contender than a so-called superstar on a bad team."

DETROIT PISTON **RICHARD HAMILTON**

"Sport is the only
profession I know of
that, when you retire,
you have to go to work."

NBA HALL OF FAMER EARL "THE PEARL" MONROE

"Team has to come first. You have to care about each other more than you care about yourself. If you care about the guy to your left and the guy to your right more than you care about yourself, you know who's going to get taken care of? The guy in the middle."

TORONTO RAPTORS COACH **SAM MITCHELL**

"Sometimes a player's greatest challenge is coming to grips with his role on the team."

CHICAGO BULLS STAR **SCOTTIE PIPPEN**

"It's so bad that the players are giving each other high fives when they hit the rim."

SOUTHEASTERN MISSOURI UNIVERSITY COACH **RON SHUMATEON** ON HIS TEAM'S POOR SHOOTING

"Fans never fall asleep at our games because they're afraid they might get hit by a pass."

LONGTIME NCAA COACH **GEORGE RAVELING**

"The way we're playing, it doesn't matter who comes back. Jesus Christ could come back, and we still wouldn't have a chance."

LOS ANGELES LAKERS COACH **PHIL JACKSON** AFTER A BLOWOUT LOSS TO THE DALLAS MAVERICKS

"We were afraid we'd get arrested for impersonating a basketball team."

TULANE COACH ROY DANFORTH ON WHY HIS TEAM GOT OUT OF PHILADELPHIA
SO FAST AFTER A LOSS TO PENN

"A tough day at the office is even tougher when your office contains spectator seating."

NEW ZEALAND BASKETBALL COACH NIK POSA

"I've been watching you guys and you made me sick."

SACRAMENTO KINGS ASSISTANT COACH (AND FORMER NBA STAR)
WILLIS REED TELLS PLAYERS WHY HE WAS FEELING ILL

"They all want to give me bad players, and I've got enough of those."

ATLANTA HAWKS GENERAL MANAGER STAN KASTEN EXPLAINING
WHY HE WAS HAVING DIFFICULTY MAKING TRADES

"People like me."

SEATTLE SUPERSONICS CENTER DENNIS AWTREY EXPLAINS WHY HE HAD BEEN TRADED
SIX TIMES IN EIGHT YEARS

"I'm tired of hearing my name in trade rumors. It's time for me to move on."

PHOENIX SUNS ALL-STAR SHAWN MARION DEMANDING A TRADE
BECAUSE HE WAS TIRED OF ALL THE TRADE RUMORS ABOUT HIM

"Because my grandma said I have to."

PHILADELPHIA 76ERS STAR **CHARLES BARKLEY** ON WHY HE PLANNED TO RETURN TO AUBURN
TO EARN CREDITS TOWARD HIS DEGREE DESPITE EARNING $2 MILLION A SEASON

"One year I was like 'I need to go back and see how close I
am to graduating.' I started adding up all my credits, and I
asked the guy, 'What am I?' He says, 'You're a freshman.'"

NBA STAR TURNED BROADCASTER **CHARLES BARKLEY**

"I can't miss class. The professor doesn't have to call the roll
to know I'm not there."

NORTH CAROLINA STATE'S 7-FOOT-4 **TOM BURLESON**

"I don't know why people question the academic training of
a student athlete. Half the doctors in the country graduated
in the bottom half of their class."

MARQUETTE COACH **AL MCGUIRE**

"No, but they gave me one anyway."

LOS ANGELES LAKERS FORWARD **ELDEN CAMPBELL**,
WHEN ASKED IF HE HAD EARNED HIS DEGREE FROM CLEMSON

"I basically majored in basketball."

PHOENIX SUNS STAR **STEVE NASH**, WHO STUDIED SOCIOLOGY AT SANTA CLARA UNIVERSITY

"Ball handling and dribbling are my strongest weaknesses."

DENVER NUGGETS STAR DAVID THOMPSON

"Strength is my biggest weakness."

NEW MEXICO UNIVERSITY PLAYER MARK SNOW

"I don't like going to my right, but nobody knows that."

CONNECTICUT SUN FORWARD KATIE DOUGLAS OF THE WNBA

"The places where I need the most work are on my inside
and outside games."

KANSAS CITY KING DARNELL HILLMAN

"Winning takes talent, to repeat takes character."

UCLA COACHING STAR JOHN WOODEN

"It never gets old. It only gets old if you lose."

BOSTON CELTICS GREAT JOHN HAVLICEK ON WINNING CHAMPIONSHIPS

"I don't know what it feels like to wear a thong, but I imagine it feels something like what we had on in the first half. I feel violated."

LOS ANGELES LAKERS SUPERSTAR KOBE BRYANT AFTER THE LAKERS WORE THROWBACK JERSEYS AND SHORT-SHORTS IN A GAME AGAINST THE BOSTON CELTICS (WHO WORE THEIR REGULAR SHORTS AND ONLY THE THROWBACK JERSEYS) DURING THE 2007-08 SEASON

"Prepare for every game like you just lost your last one."

LONGTIME NBA AND NCAA COACH LON KRUGER

"Relax? How can anybody relax and play golf? You have to grip the club, don't you?"

GOLF GREAT **BEN HOGAN**

"It is impossible to outplay an opponent you can't outthink."
LAWSON LITTLE

"I always said you have to be really smart or really dumb to play this game well. I just don't know where I fit in."
BETH DANIEL

"Golf is a game that is played on a five-inch course – the distance between your ears."
GOLF LEGEND BOBBY JONES

"The worst club in my bag is my brain."
CHRIS PERRY

"Let's face it, 95 percent of this game is mental. A guy plays lousy golf he doesn't need a pro, he needs a shrink."
SPORTSWRITER TOM MURPHY

"Someone once asked him what was tougher, football or golf. He said golf because in football you just react. In golf, there's too much time to think."
BOBBY GENOVESE, ON HIS FATHER BOBBY CUNNINGHAM JR. WHO PLAYED IN THE CANADIAN FOOTBALL LEAGUE IN THE 1940S AND 50S AND GOLFED PROFESSIONALLY IN CANADA AND THE UNITED STATES

"A routine is not a routine if you have to think about it."
DAVIS LOVE JR.

"Golf combines two favorite American pastimes: taking long walks and hitting things with a stick."

POLITICAL SATIRIST **P.J. O'ROURKE**

"Golf is good for the soul. You get so mad at yourself you forget to hate your enemies."

HUMORIST **WILL ROGERS**

"They throw their clubs backwards, and that's wrong. You should always throw a club ahead of you so that you don't have to walk any extra distance to get it."

TOMMY BOLT ON THE TEMPERS OF OTHER PLAYERS

"Why do we work so hard to feel so terrible?"

HOLLIS STACY

"You must never forget that golf is supposed to be a game of relaxation. It should take your mind off your work, your mortgage, your income tax and introduce fresh and much more serious problems into your life."

STEPHEN BAKER

"If I ever needed an eight foot putt, and everything I owned depended on it, I would want Arnold Palmer to putt for me."

GOLF LEGEND **BOBBY JONES**

"Nicklaus may be the only pro in the world who can frighten other pros with his practice shots."

AUTHOR AND BROADCASTER **DICK SCHAAP**

"I can sum it up like this: Thank God for the game of golf."
ARNOLD PALMER

"Watching the Masters on CBS is like attending a church service. Announcers speak in hushed, pious tones, as if to convince us that something of great meaning and historical importance is taking place. What we are actually seeing is grown men hitting little balls with sticks."
TOM GILMORE

"The first time I played the Masters, I was so nervous I drank a bottle of rum before I teed off. I shot the happiest 83 of my life."
CHI CHI RODRIGUEZ

"Golf is so popular simply because it is the best game in the world at which to be bad."
BRITISH AUTHOR A.A. MILNE, BEST KNOWN FOR HIS BOOKS ABOUT WINNIE THE POOH

"I like golf because you can be really terrible at it and still not look much dorkier than anybody else."
HUMOR COLUMNIST DAVE BARRY

"My clubs are well used, but unfortunately not used well."
JACK BURRELL

"It is the constant and undying hope for improvement that makes golf so exquisitely worth playing."

"I don't think of myself as a celebrity or superstar. I'm just an ordinary guy who makes his living in a crazy way. My only fear is that I may have to go out and get a real job."

FUZZY ZOELLER

"I love to play. I love fishing and hunting and trapshooting and ping-pong and chess and pool and billiards and driving a motor-car, and at times I love golf, when I can get the shots going somewhere near the right. It seems I love almost any pursuit ... except work."

BOBBY JONES

"My golf is woeful but I will never surrender."

ENTERTAINER AND GOLF ENTHUSIAST **BING CROSBY**

"My wife said to me the other day, 'My God, you may get to 65 without ever working a day in your life.'"

JOHN BRODIE, AFTER JOINING THE SENIOR TOUR

"When I ask you what club to hit, look the other way and don't you dare say a word."

ADVICE FROM GOLF LEGEND **SAM SNEAD** TO HIS CADDY

"I'm about five inches from being an outstanding golfer. That's the distance my left ear is from my right."

BEN CRENSHAW

"Always remember that however good you may be, the game is your master."

J.H. TAYLOR

"The more you play it the less you know about it."

LPGA LEGEND **PATTY BERG**

"One thing about golf is you don't know why you play bad and why you play good."

GEORGE ARCHER

"One minute you're bleeding. The next minute you're hemorrhaging. The next minute you're painting the Mona Lisa."

MAC O'GRADY, DESCRIBING A TYPICAL ROUND OF GOLF

"Golf is a spiritual game. It's like Zen. You have to let your mind take over."

AMY ALCOTT

"When I make a bad shot, your job is to take the blame."

ADVICE FROM **SEVE BALLESTEROS** TO HIS CADDIES

"Golf is an awkward set of bodily contortions designed to produce a graceful result."

TOMMY ARMOUR

"The ideal build for a golfer would be strong hands, big forearms, thin neck, big thighs and a flat chest. He'd look like Popeye."

GARY PLAYER

"If God wants to produce the ideal golfer then He should create a being with a set of unequal arms and likewise legs, an elbow-free left arm, knees which hinge sideways and a ribless torso from which emerges, at an angle of 45 degrees, a stretched neck fitted with one color-blind eye stuck firmly on the left side."

GOLF WRITER CHRIS PLUMRIDGE

"Caddies are a breed of their own. If you shoot 66, they say, 'Man, we shot 66!' But go out and shoot 77 and they say, 'Hell, he shot 77!'"

LEE TREVINO

"Golf asks something of a man. It makes one loathe mediocrity. It seems to say, 'If you are going to keep company with me, don't embarrass me.'"

SOUTH AFRICAN STAR **GARY PLAYER**

"The man who can go into a patch of rough alone, with the knowledge that only God is watching him, and play his ball where it lies, is the man who will serve you faithfully and well."

ENGLISH COMIC WRITER **P.G. WODEHOUSE**

"Eighteen holes of match or medal play will teach you more about your foe than will 18 years of dealing with him across a desk."

LEGENDARY SPORTSWRITER **GRANTLAND RICE**

"Confidence is everything. From there, it's a small step to winning."

CRAIG STADLER

"It takes hundreds of good golf shots to gain confidence, but only one bad one to lose it."

JACK NICKLAUS

"A lot of people think I am cold and have no feelings. But I do. I just try very hard to focus and not let my emotions take over on the golf course."

ANNIKA SORENSTAM

"Talking to a golf ball won't do you any good, unless you do it while your opponent is teeing off."

AUTHOR BRUCE LANSKY

"You can't call it a sport. You don't run, jump, you don't shoot, you don't pass. All you have to do is buy some clothes that don't match."

BASEBALL PLAYER STEVE SAX

"To play golf you need goofy pants and a fat ass."

ACTOR ADAM SANDLER AS HAPPY GILMORE

"'Play it as it lies' is one of the fundamental dictates of golf. The other is 'Wear it if it clashes.'"

HUMORIST HENRY BEARD

"Although golf was originally restricted to wealthy, overweight Protestants, today it's open to anybody who owns hideous clothing."

HUMOR WRITER DAVE BARRY

"When you get up there in years, the fairways get longer and the holes get smaller."

SOUTH AFRICAN GOLF STAR BOBBY LOCKE

"The older you get, the easier it is to shoot your age."

JERRY BARBER

"That's the easiest 69 I ever made."

WALTER HAGEN, ON TURNING 69

"The older I get, the better I used to be."

LEE TREVINO

"You know you're on the Senior Tour when your back goes out more than you do."

BOB BRUCE

"That's life. The older you get, the tougher it is to score."

COMEDIAN BOB HOPE

"What's nice about our tour is you can't remember your bad shots."

BOB BRUCE, ON THE SENIOR TOUR

"Around a clubhouse they'll tell you even God has to practice his putting. In fact, even Nicklaus does."

LEGENDARY SPORTSWRITER JIM MURRAY

"The older you get the stronger the wind gets ... and it's always in your face."

JACK NICKLAUS

"When he plays well, he wins. When he plays badly, he finishes second. When he plays terribly, he finishes third."

JOHNNY MILLER ON JACK NICKLAUS

"Golf is like a love affair. If you don't take it seriously, it's no fun; if you do take it seriously, it breaks your heart."

ENGLISH WRITER ARNOLD DALY

"One hundred years of experience has demonstrated that the game is temporary insanity practiced in a pasture."

SPORTSWRITER DAVE KINDRED

"Playing golf is like chasing a quinine pill around a cow pasture."

SIR WINSTON CHURCHILL

"Golf is, in part, a game; but only in part. It is also in part a religion, a fever, a vice, a mirage, a frenzy, a fear, an abscess, a joy, a thrill, a pest, a disease, an uplift, a brooding, a melancholy, a dream of yesterday, and a hope for tomorrow."

NEW YORK TRIBUNE (1916)

"Golf is typical capitalist lunacy."
PLAYWRIGHT GEORGE BERNARD SHAW

"Golf is just a game — and an idiotic game most of the time."
MARK CALCAVECCHIA

"Golf is an insurmountable game in which one attempts to put an insignificant ball into an obscure hole with an absurd weapon."
HARRY B. TROUT

"Golf is a lot of walking, broken up by disappointment and bad arithmetic.
JOURNALIST EARL WILSON

"Golf seems to me an arduous way to go for a walk. I prefer to take the dogs out."
PRINCESS ANNE OF ENGLAND

"Golf is a good walk spoiled."
AUTHOR MARK TWAIN

"Golf tips are like aspirins. One may do you good, but if you swallow the whole bottle you will be lucky to survive."
GOLF COACH HARVEY PENICK

"SOMETIMES THINGS DON'T GO YOUR WAY, AND THAT'S THE WAY THINGS GO."

TIGER WOODS

"I don't trust doctors. They are like golfers. Every one has a different answer to your problem."

SEVE BALLESTEROS

"I have a tip that can take five strokes off anyone's golf game: it's called an eraser."

ARNOLD PALMER

"Golf is the most over-taught and least-learned human endeavor. If they taught sex the way they teach golf, the race would have died out years ago."

LEGENDARY SPORTSWRITER JIM MURRAY

"If you can hit the ball in the hole regularly by standing on your head, then keep right on — and don't listen to advice from anyone."

ENGLISH GOLF PRO JOHN JACOBS

"The difference between a sand trap and water is the difference between a car crash and an airplane crash. You have a chance of recovering from a car crash."

BOBBY JONES

"Golf balls are attracted to water as unerringly as the eye of a middle-aged man to a female bosom."

WRITER MICHAEL GREEN

"I owe a lot to my parents, especially my mother and my father."

GREG NORMAN

"The way I putted, I must have been reading the greens in Spanish and putting them in English."

HOMERO BLANCAS

"After all these years, it's still embarrassing for me to play on the American golf tour. Like the time I asked my caddy for a sand wedge and he came back ten minutes later with a ham on rye."

PUERTO RICAN STAR CHI CHI RODRIQUEZ ON HIS ACCENT

"My career started off slowly and then tapered off."

GARY MCCORD

"He must be amphibious."

BRITISH GOLFER MARK JAMES AFTER SERGIO GARCIA THREW A BALL INTO THE GALLERY WITH HIS LEFT HAND

"I play in the low 80s. If it's any hotter than that, I won't play."

COMEDIAN JOE E. LEWIS

"OF ALL THE HAZARDS, FEAR IS THE WORST."

GOLF LEGEND SAM SNEAD

> **"I'm hitting the woods just great ... but I'm having a terrible time getting out of them."**
>
> HARRY TOSCANO

"One under a tree, one under a bush, one under the water."

LEE TREVINO, DESCRIBING HOW HE WAS ONE UNDER DURING A TOURNAMENT

"I'd like to see the fairways more narrow. Then everybody would have to play from the rough, not just me."

SEVE BALLESTEROS

"A rough should have high grass. When you go bowling they don't give you anything for landing in the gutter, do they?"

LEE TREVINO

"What goes up must come down. But don't expect it to come down where you can find it."

COMEDIAN LILY TOMLIN

"A golf ball is like a clock. Always hit it at 6 o'clock and make it go toward 12 o'clock. But make sure you're in the same time zone."

CHI CHI RODRIGUEZ

"Golf is not a game of good shots. It's a game of bad shots."

GOLF LEGEND BEN HOGAN

"Forget your opponents. Always play against par."

SAM SNEAD

"The best wood in most amateurs' bags is the pencil."

CHI CHI RODRIQUEZ

"Art said he wanted to get more distance. I told him to hit it and run backward."

KEN VENTURI, ON THE ADVICE HE GAVE TO LONGTIME SPORTSWRITER ART ROSENBAUM

"Bob Hope has a beautiful short game. Unfortunately, it's off the tee."

JIMMY DEMARET

"You've just one problem. You stand too close to the ball ... after you've hit it."

SAM SNEAD

"They call it golf because all the other four letter words were taken."

RAYMOND FLOYD

"I used to go to the driving range to practice driving without slicing. Now I go to the driving range to practice slicing without swearing."

AUTHOR BRUCE LANSKY

"If profanity had an influence on the flight of the ball, the game of golf would be played far better than it is."

ENGLISH GOLF WRITER HORACE G. HUTCHINSON

"I was afraid to move my lips in front of the TV cameras. The commissioner probably would have fined me just for what I was thinking."

TOM WEISKOPF, AFTER SHOOTING A 13 ON THE TWELFTH HOLE DURING THE 1980 MASTERS

"Golf is a game of expletives not deleted."

DR. IRVING A. GLADSTONE

"My divorce came as a complete surprise. That's what happens when you haven't been home in 18 years."

LEE TREVINO

"Someone once told me that there is more to life than golf. I think it was my ex-wife."

AUTHOR BRUCE LANSKY

"MY MAIN GOAL STARTING THE DAY WAS TO GO OUT THERE AND WIN THE GOLF TOURNAMENT."

VIJAY SINGH

"If I had to choose between my wife and my putter ... well, I'd miss her."

GARY PLAYER

"Don't play too much golf. Two rounds a day are plenty."

HARRY VARDON

"I play golf with friends sometimes, but there are never friendly games."

BEN HOGAN

"When you are ahead, don't take it easy. Kill them. After the finish, then be a sportsman."

EARL WOODS TO HIS SON TIGER

"I never rooted against an opponent, but I never rooted for him either."

ARNOLD PALMER

"Golf is a game in which you yell 'Fore,' shoot six, and write down five."

BROADCASTER PAUL HARVEY

"If there is any larceny in a man, golf will bring it out."

WRITER PAUL GALLICO

"Golf is a game in which the ball lies poorly and the players well."

SPORTSWRITER ART ROSENBAUM

"Golf is the hardest game in the world to play, and the easiest to cheat at."

DAVE HILL

"I can airmail the golf ball, but sometimes I don't put the right address on it."

JIM DENT, WHO WAS THE LONGEST HITTER ON THE PGA TOUR BUT NOT THE MOST ACCURATE

"Drive for show, but putt for dough."

BOBBY LOCKE

"My favorite shots are the practice swing and the conceded putt. The rest can never be mastered."

ONETIME BRITISH DEFENSE SECRETARY AND NATO SECRETARY-GENERAL LORD ROBERTSON

"Golf is the hardest game in the world. There is no way you can ever get it. Just when you think you do, the game jumps up and puts you in your place."

BEN CRENSHAW

"That's as bad as getting back together with an ex-wife."

JOHN DALY, WHO'S NOW BEEN DIVORCED FOUR TIMES, AFTER A POOR SHOT AT THE 2006 TELUS SKINS GAME IN BANFF, ALBERTA

"His driving is unbelievable. I don't go that far on my holidays."

IAN BAKER-FINCH, ON JOHN DALY

"Grip it and rip it. It works for John Daly. It never worked for me. All I did was wear out golf gloves."

WRITER/EDITOR CHUCK STARK

"I enjoy the oohs! and aahs! from the gallery when I hit my drives. But I'm getting pretty tired of the awws! and uhhs! when I miss the putt."

JOHN DALY

"No one has ever conquered this game. One week out there and you are God, next time you are the devil. But it does keep you coming back."

JULI INKSTER

"I have always had a drive that pushes me to try for perfection, and golf is a game in which perfection stays just out of reach."

LPGA GREAT BETSY RAWLS

"The only stats I care about are paychecks and victories."

GREG NORMAN

"Victory is everything. You can spend the money, but you can never spend the memories."

KEN VENTURI

"I never wanted to be a millionaire. I just wanted to live like one."

WALTER HAGEN

"The world's number one tennis player spends 90 percent of his time winning, while the world's number one golfer spends 90 percent of his time losing. Golfers are great losers."

IRISH GOLFER DAVID FEHERTY

"I did not ever dream in my wildest imagination there would be as much money or that people would hit the ball so far. I only won $182,000 in my whole life. In 1937, I got fifth-place money at the British Open — $187 — and it cost me $3,000 to play because I had to take a one-month leave of absence from my club job to go."

BYRON NELSON

"To be truthful, I think golfers are overpaid. It's unreal, and I have trouble dealing with the guilt sometime."

COLIN MONTGOMERIE

"I'm playing pretty good now, but my ranking doesn't say that. I'm number two."

VIJAY SINGH

"It's a heck of a lot harder to stay on top than it is to get there."

TOM KITE

"Nobody ever remembers who finished second at anything."

JACK NICKLAUS

"The object of golf is to beat someone. Make sure that someone is not yourself."

BOBBY JONES

"You need a fantastic memory in this game to remember the great shots and a very short memory to forget the bad ones."

MAC O'GRADY

"The mind messes up more shots than the body."

TOMMY BOLT

"In golf, as in no other sport, your principal opponent is yourself."

LEGENDARY SPORTSWRITER HERBERT WARREN WIND

"If you're caught on a golf course during a storm and are afraid of lightning, hold up a one-iron. Not even God can hit a one-iron."

LEE TREVINO

"Actually, the only time I ever took out a one-iron was to kill a tarantula. And I took a seven to do that."

LEGENDARY SPORTSWRITER JIM MURRAY

"The one-iron is almost unplayable. You keep it in your bag the way you keep a Dostoyevsky novel in your bookcase — with the vague notion that you will try it someday. In the meantime, it impresses your friends."

GOLF WRITERS TOM SCOTT AND GEOFFREY COUSINS

"A good one-iron shot is about as easy to come by as an understanding wife."

WRITER DAN JENKINS

"It's a lot easier hitting a quarterback than a little white ball."

HALL OF FAME DEFENSIVE LINEMAN BUBBA SMITH

"I was three over.
One over a house, one over a patio,
and one over a swimming pool."

BASEBALL HALL OF FAMER GEORGE BRETT

"It took me seventeen years to get 3,000 hits in baseball. I did it in one afternoon on the golf course."

BASEBALL HALL OF FAMER HANK AARON

"But you don't have to go up in the stands and play your foul balls. I do."

SAM SNEAD, TO BASEBALL GREAT TED WILLIAMS DURING AN ARGUMENT AS TO WHETHER IT WAS MORE DIFFICULT TO HIT A MOVING BASEBALL OR A STATIONARY GOLF BALL

"I think golf is good for boxing, but the reverse is far from the case."

MAX BAER, HEAVYWEIGHT CHAMPION IN THE MID 1930S

"When you're just not very good at something, it's sometimes hard to justify spending six hours to do it."

SIX-TIME TOUR DE FRANCE CYCLING CHAMPION LANCE ARMSTRONG ON GOLF

"One of the advantages bowling has over golf is that you seldom lose a bowling ball."

BOWLING LEGEND DON CARTER

301

"It's the most humbling sport ever. It's like a lousy lover. It's like some guy who's never there when you need him. Every once in a while, he comes and makes you feel like heaven on earth. And then the moment you say, **'I really need this,' he's gone."**

ENTERTAINER AND GOLF ENTHUSIAST DINAH SHORE

"Every shot counts. The three-foot putt is just as important as the 300-yard drive."

LEGENDARY BRITISH GOLFER HENRY COTTON

"Be decisive. A wrong decision is generally less disastrous than indecision."

BERNHARD LANGER

"If you can't outplay them, outwork them."

BEN HOGAN

"Keep close count of your nickels and dimes, stay away from whiskey, and never concede a putt."

SAM SNEAD

"They say golf is like life, but don't believe them. Golf is more complicated than that."

LONGTIME PGA PRO AND SENIOR TOUR FOUNDER GARDNER DICKINSON

"Golf is deceptively simple, yet endlessly complicated."

ARNOLD PALMER

"Golf giveth and golf taketh away, but it taketh away a hell of a lot more than it giveth."

SOUTH AFRICAN GOLFER SIMON HOBDAY

"I know I am getting better at golf because I'm hitting fewer spectators."

PRESIDENT GERALD FORD

"Whenever I play with Gerald Ford, I try to make it a foursome — the President, myself, a paramedic and a faith healer."

COMEDIAN BOB HOPE

"I would like to deny all allegations by Bob Hope that during my last game of golf, I hit an eagle, a birdie, an elk and a moose."

GERALD FORD

"President Eisenhower has given up golf for painting. It takes fewer strokes."

BOB HOPE

"Watching Sam Snead practice hitting golf balls is like watching a fish practice swimming."

JOHN SCHLEE

"Practice puts brains in your muscles."

SAM SNEAD

"Swing hard
in case you hit it."
HALL OF FAME QUARTERBACK DAN MARINO

"It's a funny thing, the more I practice the luckier I get."
ARNOLD PALMER

"What a shame to waste those great shots on the practice tee."
WALTER HAGEN

"There are two things you can do with your head down — play golf and pray."
LEE TREVINO

"Some of us worship in churches, some in synagogues, some on golf courses."
AMERICAN POLITICIAN ADLAI STEVENSON

"If you call on God to improve the results of a shot while it is still in motion, you are using 'an outside agency' and are subject to appropriate penalties under the rules of the game."
ENGLISH GOLF WRITER HENRY LONGHUST

"No golfer can ever become too good to practice."
LEGENDARY BRITISH LADIES CHAMPION MAY HEZLET

"Baseball players quit playing and they take up golf. Basketball players quit, take up golf. Football players quit, take up golf. What are we supposed to take up when we quit?"

GEORGE ARCHER

"I'm gambling that when we get into the next life, Saint Peter will look at us and ask, 'Golfer?' And when we nod, he will step aside and say, 'Go right in; you've suffered enough.' One warning, if you do go in and the first thing you see is a par 3 surrounded by water, it ain't heaven."

LEGENDARY SPORTSWRITER JIM MURRAY

"Putts get real difficult the day they hand out the money."

LEE TREVINO

"Pressure is playing for $10 when you don't have a dime in your pocket."

LEE TREVINO

"I've heard people say putting is 50 percent technique and 50 percent mental. I really believe it is 50 percent technique and 90 percent positive thinking. See, but that adds up to 140 percent, which is why nobody is 100 percent sure how to putt."

CHI CHI RODRIGUEZ

"I've never been to heaven, and thinking back on my life, I probably won't get a chance to go. I guess the Masters is as close as I'm going to get."

FUZZY ZOELLER AFTER WINING THE 1979 MASTERS

"Half of golf is fun. The other half is putting."

BRITISH GOLF COLUMNIST PETER DOBEREINER

"Retire to what? I'm a golfer and a fisherman.
I've got no place to retire to."

JULIUS BOROS

"Playing golf is a little like carving a turkey. It helps if you
have your slice under control."

HUMORIST BOB ORBEN

"I don't say my golf game is bad, but if I grew tomatoes
they'd come up sliced."

MILLER BARBER

"It's so bad I could putt off a tabletop and still leave the ball
halfway down the leg."

J.C. SNEAD

"If I had hit it like I wanted to I'd have holed it."

MARK CALCAVECCHIA

"Every week."

JEFF SLUMAN, KNOWN AS A SHORT HITTER, WHEN ASKED IF HE'S EVER PLAYED A COURSE HE
THOUGHT WAS TOO LONG

"Because the other one didn't float."

"How did I make a twelve on a par five hole? It's simple. I missed a four-foot-putt for an eleven."

ARNOLD PALMER

"The golf swing is like a suitcase into which we are trying to pack one too many things. "

WRITER JOHN UPDIKE

"Golf swings are like snowflakes: there are no two exactly alike."

PETER JACOBSEN

"Reverse every natural instinct and do the opposite of what you are inclined to do, and you will probably come very close to having a perfect golf swing."

BEN HOGAN

"Dividing the swing into its parts is like dissecting a cat. You'll have blood and guts and bones all over the place. But you won't have a cat."

BRITISH GOLFER ERNEST JONES WHO BECAME ONE OF THE GAME'S FIRST GREAT INSTRUCTORS

"My handicap? Woods and irons."
BASEBALL PLAYER CHRIS CODIROLI

"The point is that it doesn't matter if you look like a beast before or after the hit, as long as you look like a beauty at the moment of impact."
SEVE BALLESTEROS

"The only thing you should force in a golf swing is the club back into the bag."
BYRON NELSON

"I get way more nervous playing golf in front of 500 people than being on stage in front of 20,000 people."
SINGER JUSTIN TIMBERLAKE

"One day I did get angry with myself and threw a club. My caddy told me, 'You're not good enough to get mad.'"
ACTOR SAMUEL L. JACKSON

"Golf takes me out of the crap of a sick world. Golfers are genuinely courteous in a discourteous world. Show me a guest on The Jerry Springer Show who's a golfer."
ACTOR JAMES WOODS

"I don't know why that **putt hung** on the edge. I'm a **clean liver.** **It must be my caddy.99**

JOANNE CARNER

"It was cool for a couple of weeks, but how much bad golf can you play?"

ACTOR JOHN GOODMAN

"The real reason your pro tells you to keep your head down is so you can't see him laughing at you."

COMEDIAN PHYLLIS DILLER

"I putted like Joe Schmoe, and I'm not even sure Joe would appreciate that."

ARNOLD PALMER AFTER A BAD ROUND

"I've always played all right when I've played with him. I think it's very easy to get caught up watching him play because it's so much fun. All of a sudden you're on the sixth hole and haven't really paid attention to what you're doing."

2006 U.S. OPEN CHAMPION GEOFF OGILVY ON PLAYING WITH TIGER WOODS

"I always feel pressure. If you don't feel nervous, that means you don't care about how you play. I care about how I perform. I've always said the day I'm not nervous playing is the day I quit."

TIGER WOODS

"Miles and miles and miles."

ALAN SHEPARD DESCRIBING THE FLIGHT OF HIS SECOND GOLF SHOT ON THE MOON

"My game is so bad I gotta hire three caddies: one to walk the left rough, one for the right rough, and one down the middle. And the one in the middle doesn't have much to do."

DAVE HILL

"My luck is so bad that if I bought a cemetery people would stop dying."

ED FURGOL

"If I'm on the course and lightning starts, I get inside fast. If God wants to play through, let him."

COMEDIAN BOB HOPE

"You hear that winning breeds winning. But no, winners are bred from losing. They learn they don't like it."

TOM WATSON

"A great round of golf is like a terrible round. You drift into a zone, and it's hard to break out of it."

AL GEIBERGER

"**Show me a man who is a good loser** and **I'll show you** a man who is playing golf with **his boss.**"

LEGENDARY SPORTSWRITER JIM MURRAY

I played golf with a priest the other day.
He shot par-par-par-par-par.
Finally I said to him,

'Father, if you're
   playing golf like this
you haven't been
            saving many
            souls lately.'

SAM SNEAD